To Cynthia Burdock
on her birthday,
with fond wishes.

— Tom Hogan
8 August 1995

Amateur at the Keyboard

Amateur at the Keyboard

A Practice and Study Guide for Nonprofessional Pianists

by
JAMES HIGSON

McFarland & Company, Inc., Publishers
Jefferson, North Carolina, and London

I am sincerely indebted to G. Henle Verlag of Munich for kind permission to reproduce a number of examples directly from their splendid collection of major works for the piano. All examples are referenced in the index. —*J.H.*

British Library Cataloguing-in-Publication data are available

Library of Congress Cataloguing-in-Publication Data

Higson, James, 1925–
    Amateur at the keyboard : a practice and study guide for nonprofessional pianists / by James Higson.
      p. cm.
    Includes discography (p. 193) and index.
    ISBN 0-89950-589-9 (lib. bdg. : 50# alk. paper) ∞
    1. Piano — Methods — Self-instruction. I. Title.
MT248.H53 1991
786.2′193 — dc20   90-53498
                                             CIP
                                             MN

Manufactured in the United States of America

McFarland & Company, Inc., Publishers
  Box 611, Jefferson, North Carolina 28640

For my good piano friends,
John C. Hecht and Robert C. Dick

Contents

Introduction

This book is aimed directly at busy people who have either had some early piano or musical training or whose exposure to music causes them to want to expand that interest and give it a larger share of their lives.

How would you react if you were told that you could pursue the study of the piano by

- forgetting about wrong notes,
- never practicing exercises or scales,
- never performing in a recital,
- never using a metronome,
- playing at fairly slow speeds and enjoying it,
- using plenty of pedal,
- splurging on a terrific piano,
- playing pieces well above your ability,
- benefiting from recordings and CDs,
- skipping the orange-squeezing hand position,
- participating in a more exhilarating life-style?

You would be skeptical about achieving any results. Yet it is just these sympathetic principles that are woven into the exciting plan of study and enjoyment that follows. My own trials with exploring the piano are part of this adventure. Lift up your chin, pull up your socks, and brace yourself for a different look at the life of a piano buff, who was no wunderkind.

Most of us harbor a naive conception that we have our hands full by pursuing a single goal aggressively. Whether it is an essential business or professional commitment or one of purely artistic and voluntary character, the thought of supplementing it with a serious secondary goal seems to be more than our daily lives and ambitions can encompass. In other words, as fully scheduled, working adults it seems unrealistic to embark on a burdensome piano objective with all the discipline, dedication of time, and effort that it entails.

Andrew Marvell's thoughts about our tendency to limit goals and remain needlessly single-purposed were beautifully expressed in his poem "The Garden":

How vainly men themselves amaze
To win the Palm, the Oke, or Bayes;
And their uncessant Labours see
Crown'd from some single Herb or Tree.
Whose short and narrow verged Shade
Does prudently their Toyles upbraid;
While all Flow'rs and all Trees do close
To weave the Garlands of repose.

A delightful scenario of vain pursuit is revealed in James McCay's *The Management of Time*, where he details the steps taken by an elderly lady as she sets about the seemingly basic task of folding a letter, placing it in an envelope, then sealing, stamping, and mailing it. After first regarding her hands, she flexes them, perhaps to assure herself that they are worthy of the endeavor. Then she withdraws the stamps and envelope from her desk, and invokes a secretive response from her salivary glands . . . well, you get the idea. She has made her single task fill an infinite void of time. These two extremes point up the same abuse of time in pursuit of a solitary goal. However, there is only so much time; it is finite and it cannot be stretched. It is up to us to divide it up so that more of it counts.

Our principal work is certainly a major commitment. Serious study of the piano is a major commitment. How can they coexist along with our recognition that anything approaching major daily practice sessions would be unrealistic? Our work would suffer and our other activities would be sacrificed. We would be tempted to give up the idea before we even got started.

No, our election here has to be a matter of hard choices and painful allocations. We must thwart Delmore Schwartz's cynical lines in his poem "All Clowns Are Masked":

. . . he who chooses chooses what is given;
He who chooses is ignorant of Choice.

Of the twenty-six equivalent meanings given for the word "amateur," in the current edition of J. I. Rodale's *The Synonym Finder*, eighteen of them have a pejorative connotation: dabbler, dallier, trifler, putterer, potterer, dilettante, beginner, novice, tyro, and so on. Whereas a Webster's *Collegiate Dictionary* of just fifty years ago gives as the principal definition, "one who is attached to, or cultivates, a particular pursuit, study, or science, *from taste* without pursuing it professionally." These meanings implied from two not-too-distant ages hardly convey the same thought.

Up to the turn of the century the members of the nobility and gentlemen of leisure were automatically amateurs at whatever they tackled and however seriously. Nobody has said that Henry VIII wrote lousy music or that the Earl of Rochester was a second-rate pornographer. However, as the burgeoning middle class found itself with increasing leisure time and unlimited opportunities for hobbies and diversions, the proliferation of ventures possible wreaked trivialization on the domain of the amateur. One man's violin was another man's kazoo.

At the age of seventy-six, Thomas Jefferson drew a map for the site of the University of Virginia, drew the plans for the buildings, surveyed the grounds, and supervised the construction of the first buildings. He trained bricklayers and carpenters on the site when skilled labor ran short, and polished things off with a system of rules for the students and a helping hand in hiring the predominantly European staff. This was amateurism of a high order, not the potterings of a dilettante.

Roland Barthes, the French literary critic, has this to say about amateurs in his book, *The Grain of the Voice:*

> What does "amateur" mean to you? . . . I paint or play music in the completely assumed role of a simple amateur. The enormous benefit of the amateur's situation is that it involves no image-repertoire, no narcissism. When one draws or paints as an amateur, there is no preoccupation with the *imago*, the image one will project of oneself in making the drawing or painting. It's thus a liberation, I would almost say a liberation from civilization. . . . A civilization where people would act without being preoccupied with the image of themselves they will project to others.

In November 1989 William F. Buckley presented on his *Firing Line* program a tribute to amateurism. As a fitting example, he played a Bach chamber work on harpsichord with baroque orchestra and followed with an encore of the Gigue from the first Partita in B-flat. Buckley noted that in the nineteenth century there were more amateur musicians in a single German state than in all of the United States today.

What I propose here is a major shift in emphasis to encourage the inclusion of a pursuit of the piano in a truly meaningful way. If there is a platitude to apply to this situation it would be that you get the greatest quantity and quality of work out of already busy people. In order to apply this to ourselves it goes without saying that there have to be agonizing choices, "for we have our gifts that interrupt our choices."

These gifts (or "givens") are, ironically, our very endowments that so confuse and restrict our choices. Left unchallenged, the habits of work, society, solitude, and sleep control every moment of our destiny and design our mask for us.

This is a book about building the piano into one's hitherto busy life. It is a book of incentive, of spirit, of doing what seems impossible. The secret is not to be ignorant or fearful of hard choices, because "the future is inexhaustible."

Chapter 1

Why Play the Piano?

> In precisely this (the "Light-World") resides the ineffable charm and the very real power of emancipation that music possesses for us men. For music is the only art whose means lie outside the light-world that has so long become coextensive with our total world, and music alone, therefore, can take us right out of this world, break up the steely tyranny of light, and let us fondly imagine that we are on the verge of reaching the soul's final secret—an illusion due to the fact that our waking consciousness is now so dominated by one sense only, so thoroughly adapted to the eye-world, that it is incapable of forming, out of impressions it receives, a world of the ear.
>
> Oswald Spengler, *The Decline of the West*, 2:8–9

Why would I, in middle age, decide to take up the piano with a vengeance? Though I had played that instrument casually all of my life, my efforts were along the line of popular standards, antiquated jazz, and occasional clumsy sight-readings of the easy classics. It was quite by chance that this life-changing commitment originated. Something about being in Paris for a few weeks had fostered a mood for shedding old ideas and assuming fresh goals. That must have set the stage. The fall air was brisk and scented with roasting chestnuts. However, the ultimate accident of fate that was to spring the trap-door into "pianomania" occurred in this way.

From an old journal I fixed the date as the fall of 1975. Those fragmentary notes read, "Oct. 23—9:00 AM, Arr. Gare St.-Lazare, Chk. into H. Pas-de-Calais." It was there in one of its tiny rooms that I first became aware of some indistinct piano music. It was barely audible but by opening the doors to a linen closet in the hall outside my door and thrusting my head well into its deepest recesses I heard,

1

through the thick masonry walls, the faintest but loveliest of six-
teenth-century keyboard melodies extended and embroidered into
endless, beguiling, difficult variations.

At the time I could only vaguely perceive that I was hearing the
famous Paganini Caprice on which Liszt, Brahms, and Rachmaninoff
all based their sets of variations. I later settled on the Brahms
Paganini Variations. My next task was to determine if the source was
live or recorded.

That filtered but stunning performance seemed too elegant, too
lush, too alive to be from a radio or phonograph. Night after night
for the better part of a week I repeatedly returned to the linen closet
wall where the sound was clearest and listened over prolonged
periods to try to verify that I was not actually hearing a record or
radio program. I longed to establish that I was hearing music that
was being performed spontaneously. After repeated hearings it
became evident by a rush or lapse of tempo, an occasional pause, a
deliberate repetition of a phrase, or an infrequent wrong note that
I was listening to a live performance. Someone of considerable
amateur accomplishment was practicing the variations every day
just after sundown. The beauty and quality of the playing were undeniable. The music was superb.

I attempted to conceptualize the unseen neighbor. My vision
was of a man rather than woman, probably instigated by the vigor
and maleness of the Brahms crashing block chords and the risks he
took with the piece. I saw him as being obsessed with the beauty of
the music he was playing, letting its creation manipulate *him*. Enraptured as I was, this picturization of such an ultimate happiness

formed in me an enduring scenic image. The Oswald Spengler quote used as the epigraph could not be more apt. I was enveloped in a colossal ecstasy.

Barely able to contain my excitement at discovering this live source, I rushed down to the desk the next morning to seek a description of my phantom pianist. "You can have heard nothing," the concierge told me a bit defensively. "The walls are of double masonry construction. No sound passes through them, no sound whatsoever." Sensing what was up I hastened to assure him with words and gestures how joyously I had received this music. "C'est magnifique," I said. As if pointing a pistol, I aimed my index finger at my ear and popped my eyes to express delirious appreciation as if my ear and not my mouth had just consumed a *crème brûlée* served up by a glowering and temperamental chef.

The concierge persisted in his bluff. He continued to mistake my question for a complaint about offensive noise. "It is impossible," he said. "You heard nothing."

For several nights after identifying the Brahms I continued to hear the music. The music moved on to Concert Etudes of Liszt, Chopin Preludes, Schumann's Kreisleriana, but the pianist invariably played some portion of the Brahms Variations. Everything he touched was rich, sophisticated, and played with gorgeous phrasing and deep emotional commitment.

As a result of my persistent questioning some meager facts gradually exited the lips of a grudging but friendly night clerk. This came about no doubt because of his late hours when he ran no danger of being overheard by the daytime office functionaries. With a somewhat conspiratorial look in his eye he confided to me that the adjacent building consisted of privately leased apartments. The one nearest my floor was rented to a man of middle age who "sometimes practiced for a little bit in the evening when he got home from work."

It ran through my mind that this so-called "little bit of relaxing practice" involved playing stupendous pieces to which a capable amateur player might well dedicate a whole lifetime.

"But never to the annoyance of our guests," the concierge was quick to add.

Are we not all able to find our Paris? To me, Paris *meant* music because of this and other lucky associations. It also resounded with the church bells, choir and organ music in Notre Dame on Sundays, street and Metro troubadours, and always the music in shops and corridors that changed with the scene and time of day. However, Paris also resonated with those private artists in the unknown private residential crannies of the city. This was the Paris of living and working people, the Paris of studying and enjoyment and inspiration.

After my return home I was inflamed with a desire to try to build into my life some sort of a musical commitment such as I had perceived in that humble hotel room. I was determined to do something about it. It was doubtful that I would ever be able to approach such pieces as seriously accessible elements of my own repertoire, although it turned out that in many cases I could. To this very day I remain motivated and committed chiefly by that first awe-inspiring Paris encounter.

If you crave some words to catapult you further into this charmed musical life, read these from Pascal's *Pensées*,

> Men are charged from childhood with the care of their honour, their wealth, their friends, ... They are overwhelmed with business, training ... and they are taught that they cannot possibly be happy unless their own health, honour, and wealth ... are in good case, and that one point lacking is enough to render them unhappy. So they are furnished with positions and business that keep them on the move from break of day.
>
> A strange way, you will say, to make them happy! What more could be done to make them unhappy? ... Simply relieve them of all these cares, for then they would see themselves, they would reflect on what they are, whence they come, and whither they are bound, ... that is why, after providing them with so much to do, we bid them use every moment of leisure in amusement and play, and be always occupied. [How empty and full of filth is the heart of man!]

In partial answer to Pascal's cry from the heart, this book is the synthesis of fifteen years of effort, partial accomplishment, and accompanying frustration in that direction. Whatever the palpable result has been, the pianistic ideal has been an inspiring one for this amateur.

The joy of attempting this fulfillment has been worth the striving. These ensuing words are set down with the idea of enabling the reader, if he chooses, to chart a similar course toward a goal truly worth seeking.

A paradoxical footnote to this initial adventure occurred several years later. After a considerable absence I had returned to the Hotel Pas-de-Calais. Naturally I listened eagerly for a night or two at the same wall at the same accustomed early evening time. I failed to hear the lovely piano sounds I so longed to experience again. I lay in wait for the same late-night concierge. He was now more bearded and more curmudgeonly than I had remembered him on my previous visits.

Confident he would cooperate more than anyone else in explaining this disturbing silence from the building next door, I asked him about the pianist who had played so devotedly every evening. Had he moved away? Was he ill? I braced for shocking news. I was ready to hear about a real tragedy. You know how it goes these days.

The clerk shook his head somberly. "No. He doesn't play any more," he said. "He has taken up jogging and has given up any interest in the piano." He spoke almost jubilantly as if possibly two problems had been solved, that of potential disturbance to the guests of the hotel and that of a renegade personality being brought to heel by the salutary mores of our time.

Jogging indeed. Perhaps the Paris pianist had stumbled across the statement in Kenkō's *Essays in Idleness* where he says "you should give up any art of which you have not become a master by the age of fifty. At that age there is no prospect that you may acquire it by hard work." I hope he didn't because had I read this philosophical advice early in the game I might never have started toward my goal, since I was in my forties when I began my serious study of the piano.

I was born into a nonmusical family, nonmusical as far as I knew, for my mother had died when I was an infant. My father was an orthodontist whose main interests were golf and baseball. Faced with several changes of schools, I never developed neighborhood playmates as other children did. As an only child I found myself alone a great deal of the time. This, combined with a tendency toward introversion, moved me to spend long hours drawing, reading, or experimenting with the piano. I first played melodies by ear and later was led into some rudimentary instruction. Whatever practicing I did was haphazard but just enough to let me know what was involved. I was aware that I had some modest musical gift and came close to what Virgil Thomson meant when he wrote, "No musician ever passes an average or normal infancy, with all that means of abundant physical exercise and a certain mental passivity."

Those very early years produced little results beyond a nodding acquaintance with "The Happy Farmer" type of thing: simple classics, basic scales, key signatures, accidentals, and fundamental rhythmic notation. This mild but very embryonic exposure to music occupied no more nor less time than any single one of my other studies, though I did like to tinker with the piano by ear and marveled at the sounds that could be produced by happenstance.

As a single professional man trying to deal with a growing, demanding child, my father sent me off to boarding school in the third grade. I found myself living almost full time at the Black-Foxe Military Institute in the heart of Los Angeles. Since my father was a widower, it was obviously easier to care for me in that way. Apparently he had no other choice.

For a while what interests I had took a back seat to midget-sized uniforms, shiny leather and brass, imitation wooden guns, marching on parade, and crisp commands to stand in various rigid postures with shoulders back and chin tucked in for interminable periods of time. Classes were small and instruction rigorous in such classic rites as penmanship, Latin, chess, and fencing. My roommates for years were Charlie Chaplin, Jr., and his brother, Sydney. Numerous daily emotional traumas resembled those experienced by so many students in the revered and reviled British public schools of this century.

Early in my incarceration I was gently guided into a music program where long-suffering Miss Davis took a special interest in me. Like most teachers of that period and stratum of learning, she promoted an annual recital both to keep her pupils on their toes and to display the results of her tutelage. Having blown something as simple as "Liebesträume" during one of her recitals, it is only now after the passage of almost fifty years that I can approach that piece with comparative calm. I do not recall how I survived subsequent recitals and may have actually blocked out these events from memory. However, the daily lessons went on joyfully and served their purpose by establishing at least the pattern of a primary piano education. From that flowed an episodic grammar school acquaintance with sporadic piano classes, recitals, practice, and occasional outside teachers.

In addition to piano, I had been experimenting with drums and related percussion instruments. The music was easy to read when you consider that all you had to do was interpret the rhythm of a single line of notes. Later, at Beverly Hills High School they had an elective class of "concert orchestra" which I was able to join, playing timpani and drums. I also checked out a school-owned trumpet and practiced enough to play one of the less important trumpet parts. Briefly I tried the French horn and made some modest progress, but was always frustrated by the need to play it backward, backward from the trumpet anyway.

While I kept improvising at the piano by ear and trying to keep up on some of the classical rudiments I had learned, some of the popular and jazz music was starting to make an impression on me. Gradually I got to know other students who played instruments and wanted to play jazz. This group of friends had instruments that included a saxophone, trumpet, clarinet, drums, and sometimes bass. From the vantage point of the keyboard, and the whole range of sounds represented, I found it natural to begin writing out some simple arrangements.

My initial attempts at arrangements, now called "charts," were made by copying orchestra parts from phonograph records. With an adjustable-speed turntable you simply slowed the records down to half speed. This allowed the retarded music to stay in the same approximate key even though it was an octave lower. You had plenty of time to write down the lead melodies and then pick apart the chords and instrument parts one by one. By going over the same grooves you just kept it up until you got the whole piece fully orchestrated.

If you wanted to take the time, you could extricate the whole orchestra score by this method. After some experience you would find yourself able to imitate the same general effect and make your own score. This tactic did not produce much originality in the early stages, but at the very least it was a shortcut to becoming a hack arranger. Thus it was that during my junior and senior years at Beverly Hills High School I wrote more and more arrangements both for a school dance band and other small groups.

Those Paganini Variations in Paris came my way at an age at which I knew quite well that skills such as tennis, golf, mathematics, languages, chess, and music are difficult to acquire. Ah, but those Variations were the magnet.

When I returned home from the trip to France I started to practice seriously. I was fairly busy and had to struggle to maintain an hour a day. It was during another trip to Paris a few years later that another event occurred that set the stage for my final commitment to the piano and one that I believe I will never voluntarily break.

I was staying at the small "l'Hôtel" on the Rue des Beaux-Arts on the Left Bank. This five-story *hôtel particulier* was where Balzac once lived, where Oscar Wilde died, and was, at one time, a particularly chic and fashionable place to stay. The atmosphere of the hotel and the neighborhood reminded me of Max Ophuls's lush romantic film of the forties, *Letter from an Unknown Woman*, about a French pianist, which used so effectively throughout Liszt's "Un Sospiro" as a theme.

In fact, this time from my room in the hotel I heard the music coming forth in the morning through an open pair of French doors. These gave onto one of the iron balconies projecting into the courtyard just a floor below me, *en face*, so to speak. This time I heard a piece that I myself had sight-read several times but played only poorly and tentatively. It was Brahms's Intermezzo Opus 118, No. 2, the sweetly melancholy one in A Major that is often combined with the No. 1 as a pair, of which James Friskin says, "One of the most melodious of the short pieces. Singing legato throughout. Musically free phrasing, with carefully adjusted rubato in places, is requisite." He had just this neighboring pianist's performances in mind when he wrote that. With no introduction, here is that ravishing theme:

Andante teneramente

Who was playing that gorgeous music? Listening was easier this time than having to poke my head into a linen closet. I was able to place a chair out on my own balcony so as not to miss a note. On subsequent days whoever it was often played the piece three times over, slowly and meticulously, moderately faster, then up to a performance speed. My answer came one day when a young man clad in a V-necked sweater and jeans stepped out onto the balcony immediately following a stunning performance of the Intermezzo. He took a breath or two of air, looked around, then retreated into the interior to practice it one more time. With each rendering he seemed to improve the phrasing and dynamic range, not over-sentimentalizing it, but merely getting increasingly more out of the composition, breathing with it, bringing out those gorgeous inner voices in the center section, exploiting its sonorities, making it organ-like and orchestral. It thrilled me to hear that simple piece repeated so painstakingly and ultimately performed with such exquisite unity and beauty.

Immediately I took a fresh vow—that the very second I returned home I would plunge into some weekly lessons, no matter what the obstacles were. Moreover, I would not only commit myself to regular, lengthy practice daily, but I would set some realistic goals and try to achieve them. If I could not hope to deal with the Paganini Variations, along with the Beethoven Sonata 111, Liszt B minor Sonata, Schumann Fantasie in C, Schubert Wanderer, all of which often elude the grasp of most amateurs, I would at least make a valiant attempt to learn the Brahms Intermezzo superbly, together with many more of the other pieces of only moderate to reasonable difficulty. I was impatient to start climbing my Everest.

The young man continued to practice twice each day faithfully, almost as if he were preparing for a specific event. He played other Brahms numbers, also the Chopin B minor Sonata, and some Eric Satie. Then one night in the dim apartment the lights were all turned up unexpectedly and the playing abruptly ceased. There were boisterous greetings as I saw that three men had come into the apartment with what appeared to be instrument cases. They had interrupted the Satie and they must have asked that he play it to the end for them. So he started again from the beginning and did. Was it to please them? Were they to play something together there or someplace else later on that night? At the conclusion of the piece they rushed from the apartment, cases and all. The lights went off as suddenly as they had come on. Was he part of a chamber group going off to give a concert? Why, then, had he not been practicing ensemble music? I never knew.

Several years later I was staying with friends who lived not too far from Rue des Beaux-Arts. I chose a morning when it was gently raining to walk down the narrow alley-like street that runs behind "l'Hôtel," Rue Visconte. As I drew near the street frontage of the very apartment building from which I knew the lovely playing had originated, I could hear the faint familiar sound of romantic piano music. Intermingled with the zip of wet tire treads ripping through the moist streets and the patting of delicate rain on my umbrella I knew that my man was still hard at his endless, timeless, spiritual task. The sound was too feeble to enable me to recognize the piece he was playing this time, but the scene was, nonetheless, perfect: Paris, rain, a romantic performer transported and fulfilled, and myself, a listener sharing a near comparable state of sublimity. Thank goodness he had not succumbed to jogging.

That is a real scene that does not have to be even vaguely imagined. It only needs to be conjured up whenever I want my playing to be elevated. If I find myself playing only to exercise the piano and merely going through the motions of an unfeeling pedestrian performance, I know it is time to call up those far-off Parisian scenes. I need only reactivate what I felt as I pressed my ear tightly to that masonry wall and heard those marvelous Brahms Variations, or reconstruct in my mind that magical courtyard as I sat on my narrow balcony and absorbed the growing perfection of that Intermezzo, or coax back those lacy fragments of pieces that enwrapped me so inescapably as I stood transfixed in a light Parisian rain on the wet cobbles of the Rue Visconte.

Charles Cooke, in his excellent book, *Playing the Piano for Pleasure*, quotes Ignace Jan Paderewski as saying, "Music should be studied for itself. The intellectual drill which music gives is of great value — there is nothing that will take its place. In addition, the study of music results in almost limitless gratification in later life in the understanding of great musical masterpieces." A similar sentiment is expressed by the young conductor John Gardiner: "Music is a profound restorative."

In my own book on building one's home, I quote Sir Henry Wotton from his *Elements of Architecture:* "In architecture as in all other operative arts, the *end* must direct the Operation. The End is to build well. Well, building hath three conditions: COMMODITIES, FIRMNESS, and DELIGHT." If the vast literature of this musical art be our COMMODITIES; if the structure and devotion of our practice be our FIRMNESS; and if our aesthetic and intellectual enjoyment be our DELIGHT, we have only to make our final commitment to achieve our bliss. Cooke again finds the right words, this time from Anton Rubinstein, when he says, "The piano is a lovely instrument. You must fall in love with it, with its sound, and then be tender with it to make it, in turn, be sweeter to you. Herein" — and here Cooke writes that he laid his hand on the piano — "lies divine beauty."

It is with that lofty intention that the amateur sits down and addresses the keyboard. May these words make his labors easier and more pleasurable.

Chapter 2

People: The Best Influences

The job of resurrecting a long-term relationship with music meant looking back, as we all must, to the influences that have made us what we are. I had made an early break with music, and after two decades here I was trying to build it back into my life again, albeit for sheer pleasure this time around.

While my high school and college years were filled with numerous talented contemporaries, the most outstanding was André Previn. André stood head and shoulders above the rest of us in raw musical talent and musical maturity. Whether it came to performing a concerto with the high school orchestra, sitting in with a dance band, or playing a solo or joining in a chamber ensemble, he was outstanding at jazz, pop, classical, chamber, or accompaniment. On one memorable occasion when our little combo was hired for a dance at a UCLA fraternity house, André played a whole set in pitch darkness, for that was the level of light intended in the "ballroom." Any concern I had about his being able to see the notes was dispelled when he explained that he was eager to try to "blind-feel" the keyboard. He didn't miss a note. His performance was a perfect case example similar to the Zen master archer succeeding in hitting a bull's-eye with a bow and arrow while blindfolded.

In Bookspan and Yockney's biography of André's childhood days in Munich, they told of his lawyer father's fervid dedication to the musical education of his son. The two used to play the four-handed duet arrangements of Beethoven's symphonies. André's father insisted that they be performed up to speed, regardless of the mistakes. Years followed at the Paris Conservatory where André was one of the youngest ever to be admitted.

At a time when I was just beginning arranging lessons with Arthur Lange, André was already working as a low-paid "apprentice" in the music department at MGM and actually writing full-fledged scores. However, beyond his musical abilities André was well read in philosophy and general literature. Compared to most of the sports-loving WASPs around him, he really knew something. Moreover, he was an excellent mimic and a truly funny person. Free of any residual natural accent, he could affect a broader and more ribald dialect than most comedians. Once, when we were sailing in front of Jascha Heifitz's house he spotted an elderly bather patting himself with water and subtly whistled Mendelssohn's Violin Concerto. "If it's Heifitz, he'll look up," he said. He had an imaginative wit based on a penetrating ironic style.

When I graduated from high school I was doing more dance band arranging and felt confident in turning out what the musical intelligentsia would have called "acceptable commercial work." Certainly it was not innovative, but it did sound like a lot of other studio music being played. Eventually I was furnishing cheap scores (now called charts) to a Santa Monica dance band led by Dick Markowitz. Once in a while on playing dates I filled in on piano and sometimes conducted my own work. Occasionally I would squeak along on a third trumpet part until my unpracticed lip swelled up and put a temporary halt to the proceedings.

By a phenomenal stroke of luck combined with the aggressive efforts of the band's older professional manager, Van Tonkins, Markowitz's dance orchestra was chosen to audition for the national advertising agency, Foote, Cone, and Belding, as the regular band to accompany Hoagy Carmichael on his new radio show on the NBC network sponsored by Safeway Stores. Dick Markowitz, now a successful composer for films and television, received an untimely draft call virtually on the eve of our opening program. It was by dint of this odd accident of timing that I took over the conducting and arranging of the program.

The traditional contract cycle in broadcasting was for thirteen weeks. Our life expectancy on that show was predicted to be very short-lived, meaning one cycle. For one thing we were scheduled directly opposite the highest rated show on radio, CBS's "Lux Radio Theatre." For another, we were just a bunch of kids—I was nineteen—and to make matters worse I was obviously a stopgap measure, having been taken on as a temporary replacement because of Markowitz's abrupt departure into the army. I was convinced each week would be my last, but due to a series of quarterly miracles we survived throughout the six thirteen-week cycles of the Hoagy Carmichael network radio show, a span of over a year and a half.

Hoagy was fun to work with—gentle, cooperative, a savvy Hoosier. He resembled a pint-sized Gary Cooper, countrified, yet suave. He sported a perpetual tan and a casual, foxy look. With his smooth iron-gray hair and a glint of mischief in his eye, he came on like a smooth piece of goods—a tough hombre to handle in a real estate deal or a bar gone hostile. Maybe the years of knocking around the music business and his Indiana roots convinced him that he was not a prima donna.

One day he made an unexpected appearance at my grandmother's house in Newport Beach. He happened to be driving to the races at Del Mar and was headed south on Pacific Coast Highway. He had just passed the Arches overpass and saw Lido Isle off to his right. Remembering that I lived there with my grandmother and having some time to spare he doubled back and found our house.

My grandmother knew who he was, of course. She was a lovable, stolid lady, a real matron type who looked a little like Dame Peggy Ashcroft. She was also a teetotaler, and Hoagy came in grasping a pint of Mellow Springs. He put it on the table first thing, something that did not seem out of line in those days when you wanted to show that you weren't a moocher; not so out of line, that is, unless the house happened to belong to my grandmother.

Tension.

I was totally seized up not knowing what was going to happen. Hoagy was also one of those men who, though never drunk in public, usually gave off a faint odor of liquor like some men do toilet water. Strained pleasantries followed. Then Hoagy wandered into the kitchen and found a glass and some ice and came back and filled it half full of bourbon. Tense frown.

He spotted the piano and winked at me with that practiced eye. Rather slyly and almost playfully he sort of sashayed—it's the only way to describe it—over and sat down as naturally as if he were in his own house. Totally relaxed and with a mere chord of introduction he sweetly sang:

> Little old lady passing by,
> Catching ev'ryone's eye,
> You have such a charming manner,
> sweet and shy.

Meltdown.

My grandmother was seventy-five, old but not ancient. That day when Hoagy sang I guess she didn't mind being called old, at least in that way, since there was no doubt that Hoagy and his Mellow Springs were going to be welcome in that house anytime they wanted to come calling again.

A few months into the show Hoagy wanted to develop some running dialogue with the orchestra pianist to help him in introducing his vocals. He was seeking an intimacy that suited his unique delivery — shades of *To Have and Have Not?* He craved some banter with his accompanist, someone who could provide a contrast to his perceived middle age and project the youthful image of the band as a whole. Our excellent band pianist, Dick Hazzard, was too mature and lacked the right speaking style. I suggested André. A meeting was arranged, and he was hired in no time at all.

As we all know from his numerous live appearances and on television, André was a delightful media performer, bright in conversation and wit. He even helped sell the product we advertised, Safeway's NuMade Mayonnaise.

The sidemen in that young band scattered far and wide after the breakup of the show: war, college, business. Many became strong musical entities on their own like Markowitz, saxmen Warne Marsh, Ronnie Lang, Bob Drasnin, and Peter Matz.

For myself, the aftermath provided some free-lance arranging, some limited scoring of some single numbers in a few low-budget films, and some background orchestrations for André when he continued in radio on "The Frank Sinatra Show" for Old Gold. The availability of more time made it possible for me to return to school full time, complete my college education, and go on to Harvard Graduate Business School.

Long after I had given up music as a career I was a television executive in Los Angeles. We were negotiating for a personality "talk" show that was on another station and featured one of the world's legendary pianists, personalities, and latter-day actors, Oscar Levant. Following a complex series of events he switched to our station for a long, twice-weekly program of guests and occasional piano pieces. As program director and former musician — and latent piano enthusiast — it became my duty and pleasure to become "involved" with Levant. H. D. Thoreau said, "Beware of enterprises that require new clothes." Oscar required new everything. In particular, very special gloves were required for his handling. His personal producer would deliver him to the studio, but once there he would require the most delicate cosseting and attention until he went on camera.

It need hardly be said that our own knock-about concert grand pianos in the broadcasting studios were unacceptable to Oscar. I recall his administering his rejection by standing about fifty feet away at the studio door, shoulders hunched, coffee and books clutched, and giving a mere backhand flick to consign the entire matter to oblivion.

We dutifully rented a choice concert Steinway grand from an outside agency that was at least less to his disliking than our battle-scarred relics. Since my office was to become a sort of holding tank, so to speak, between arrival and airtime, I also rented a small console model piano in case he wished to practice before going on the air. My office already had a couch on which he could lie down and rest, which was usually the case.

His arrival was mercifully late in the day and not usually much in advance of the 7:30 PM show time. He came supplied with many packages of cigarettes, his own coffee in a thermos already creamed, accompanied with paper cups stuffed with sugar cubes and napkins. These, plus books, papers, and all else, he held encircled in front of him with both arms clenched as if these possessions were apt to be wrenched away from him at any moment. He would gasp a bit, purse his lips in a storm-gathering manner and then in that inimitably charming voice squeeze out the inevitable, "I can't go on. I can't go on. I have to go home."

"Well, Oscar. Sit down. Have some coffee. Play a little something," I would say.

"I can't play. I can't talk. I've been sick. You don't know. I have to go home. I shouldn't be here," he would say.

"We have letters. They're good. You look terrific. Sit down. Don't play," I would say. A litany. I would have to proceed both gingerly and assertively, trying to find a way to calm him.

One night he was in a particularly anxious state. He was definitely not going on. His shoulders were hunched higher than usual, and he stirred his coffee with such agitation that he wore a hole in the bottom of the paper cup. Coffee began to dribble all over the floor. The rest he threw in my wastebasket. The humor of this did not escape him, and he broke into one of his wonderful smiles and said, "Hell, it's all right. What are you so worried about? I can barely tolerate this, but I will." Oscar maintained a small but lovely repertoire of short classic pieces. He perpetually complained that he couldn't play a thing but usually capitulated, and despite his deteriorating mental and physical condition, he performed nicely on the show. Among his best were some Gershwin, of course, plus Rachmaninoff's warm E-flat Major Prelude, Chopin's Nocturne in G Major and several mazurkas, including B-flat and B minor, Debussy's "Golliwog's Cakewalk" and "Minstrels," Mompou's "Scènes des Enfants," Godowsky's "Alt Wien," and much else. I don't know if he ever practiced these pieces, but he had such a wealth of talent that it probably didn't make any difference. He could still play beautifully when the mood struck him as being just right, and perform a song and dance number that showed even another facet of his genius.

Even though Oscar took every pill he could get his hands on and one marveled that he could function at all, he remained an incomparable raconteur and wit. As a result, the television show was a great success. Though it was aired only in Los Angeles, it received a lot of media attention. Soon he was appearing on Jack Paar's show on the network in New York: no easy matter since his neurosis about flying required that he be anesthetized, taken to the airport in an ambulance, and flown unconscious to New York, accompanied by a doctor.

Oscar wrote in his memoirs, *The Unimportance of Being Oscar*, "It seems that I am determined, by hook or crook, to be unloved." I always felt it was impossible *not* to love Oscar, although I would also agree with S. N. Behrman, who referred to Oscar's friendship as a "spiked embrace."

The popular word for the influence of these important performers is "heavy." More fully stated, the music played, discussed, and remembered from André, Hoagy, and Oscar gives a reality to what would otherwise have been theoretical study or wishful thinking. Somewhat similarly, anyone desiring to establish a base in music uses everything he hears and reads, live performances, practicing, and playing to enhance his foundation.

Chapter 3

Teachers

Any amateur needs a good teacher. Forsaking my paltry grammar school classical instruction, I displayed the customary fickleness of youth and yearned to play what used to be called Popular Piano. I must have sensed that I never would grow as a pianist or musician of any kind if I could not approach my playing more spontaneously. Thus somewhere in the transition from the eighth to ninth grades I began taking lessons from an "ear" teacher. Brad Ormsby became my first inspirational tutor.

Brad was a big, good-looking man with a full head of curly hair and the look of a matinee idol. He featured nubby tweed sports jackets, rep ties, and drove a late model Cadillac convertible. What further set him apart from any previous teachers was the fact that he was truly a "popular," play-by-ear piano teacher. He taught solely the art of improvisation and ear training. He did not rely on the written notes except for the single melody line that was printed at the top line of any standard three-staff sheet music. His routine beginning piece was the old chestnut called "Shine" ("Shine. Start with your shoesies," etc.). His experiences had proved it to be a good springboard for the eventual harmonic complexities of the likes of "April in Paris," or "All the Things You Are."

Ormsby's glib, grooved, ear method saw the student starting with any piece of stock sheet music—"Shine" in this case—and utilizing only the melody line and the printed guitar chords.

This imparted an immediate awareness of basic harmonic structure, which is the cornerstone of all improvisation. The melody was played in octaves with the middle chord notes filled in when convenient. The left hand executed a "stride bass" consisting of a bass note on the first and third beat and a chord on the second and fourth, thus alternating bass/chord/bass/chord, etc. Bass and chords were derived from the guitar symbols as C, G-7th, A-dim., etc. Later he expanded this oompah rhythm to include tenths and inversions for a more complex application of the left hand.

Right off the bat I was able to perform a plausible melody and accompanying chords for simple tunes. The system made sharp and flat keys less formidable, although three accidentals were about the limit in either direction. I was acquiring some groundwork for classical sight-reading later on, since I was eventually able to take unfamiliar music and more often than not hear the harmonic progressions in my mind as later I would be called on to do in the more complex classics.

Meanwhile I developed more confidence in myself as a player, since Ormsby pushed his students to try to learn a piece a week by his octave-melody/guitar-chord method. This was the epitome of the earlier quote from Alicia de Larrocha, that the left hand functions as the foundation of everything above it with the right hand more or less following its lead in creating melody, ornamentation, and embellishment.

This style could be monotonous at the outset where you were just whanging away with parallel melody octaves and a dumb oompah bass and chords. Later you learned to enrich the melody, fill in more chords, vary the bass through inversions, and supply ornaments and ad-libs. In a way, I had entered the kindergarten of orchestration since so much had to be furnished by the player. Also, the left-hand stride style peculiarly paved the way for the role of a dance band pianist who similarly alternates bass and treble in rudimentary scores.

Since there was no room for lower-level classical nor for ear-playing pianists in the high school band or orchestra, I took an interest in playing the various percussion instruments, that is timpani and drums. Gene Krupa and Buddy Rich were the reigning monarchs in this field. I saw both of them perform live, and it seemed that few jazz musicians since have been able to match their gymnastics, twirling sticks, snapping gum, raffishly disarranged hair, and triumphant demeanor when holding forth on stage. Rich especially exuded a flashy, cocky élan like a tennis star with a dynamite serve that made him my idol. Talk about confidence; he had it in spades.

I decided to meet the challenge of these jazz idols head-on and managed to be accepted by Hollywood's premier drum teacher at the time, Murray Spivack. Originally a New Yorker, he had come to Hollywood in the 1930s and become a leading sound technician in the film studios, later an expert in the new enlarged sound of Todd-AO. He had been a theatrical "pit" drummer in the old days in the New York legitimate theatres. His interest in drums and percussion remained high. An impressive elite of studio and big band musicians sought him out during his off hours. He was most in demand by successful natural jazz drummers who felt pressured to legitimize their trade, that is to read scores, execute traditional routines, and play a variety of percussive effects like bells, timpani, special cymbals, and not just traps. They had come to the right man: Murray could teach them all of that.

Once a week, usually in the early evening, I would make my way to the Spivack apartment in West Hollywood. I would be greeted by Mrs. Spivack and a sour little Boston bull who must have been named "Be still." Without a drum in sight and with heat cranked up to withstand the cruelest of New York winters, we two would stand facing only a rubber practice pad on a waist-high pedestal and drum away on our various "mammy-daddy" rolls, paradiddles, and ratamacues. We sight-read all kinds of things and played duets, marches, show scores, concert pieces, and, of course, jazz. Amazingly this concentration on rhythm caused my piano playing to improve. Just as Brad Ormsby's ear training and left-hand work had given me a more fluid and spontaneous approach, so had Murray's tapping out of those hundreds of sixteenth and thirty-second notes improved both my rhythmic sense and sight-reading.

In the same era as the drum lessons I was playing a variety of percussion instruments such as timpani, snare drum, bells, glockenspiel, triangles, and cymbals in the school orchestra, in addition to playing some piano with small dance groups. Since the band storeroom contained a stockpile of dented silver horns of all types, looking for all the world like Harold Hill's discards, I tried the lot. In exploring the different fingering methods I found that the family of brass instruments offered the greatest appeal to possible logical mastery. Whether it was the trumpet, trombone, or baritone horn, the basic seven-position elongation of three valves was hard to beat for simplicity of understanding. Later I worked up to playing simple trumpet parts and, briefly, French horn parts with the school orchestra and, on the side, some jazz trumpet with the dance groups.

The possibility of making some arrangements for these groups arose and started another musical adventure. My record equipment played a vital part. By slowing records down to half speed and playing them over and over I could painstakingly extract the individual orchestra parts. Thus I began to orchestrate by literally transcribing my favorite arrangements so the school dance orchestra could play them. It was only a short time before I was writing some simple scores of my own and trying a little conducting.

Some time during the last year of high school I managed a transition from one of the most impressive drum teachers to one of the most impressive arrangers, Arthur Lange. He was another transplanted New Yorker. He had come to the West Coast from being a name arranger in Gotham and was now active in scoring films at Twentieth Century–Fox. Moreover, he had also invented a whole system of orchestration. Onto the manuscript of the score he would apply penciled colors that were pertinent to the various instruments of the full symphonic orchestra. His reference base was an elaborate and complicated chart that set forth all of these color designations in a massive configuration of multishaded horizontal bars that looked like a work schedule for subcontractors doing a high rise. The spectrum or rainbow progression of harmonious colors in these bars was exactly what it suggested, a visual gauge of tonal compatibility. It was appropriately called the "Spectrotone" system. By using his chart and a complete set of colored pencils, it was actually possible to study a score and analyze its harmoniousness by assigning specific colors to every note written and, depending on the instrument and range in which it was playing, judging how they blended visually. A bright green showing up in a miasma of mauve and indigo would be cause for review unless that was the effect desired.

Sessions with Arthur Lange had a dramatic impact. He lived high in the expatriate haven of the Hollywood Hills. The house, at first unseen, was approached through a gate and small motor court. It sprawled squatly on a snug ledge looking out over the city stretched below and the Pacific Ocean and Catalina beyond. I would enter an immense living room which contained two grand pianos. Lange wore earth-girdling spectacles that were the first of the giant lens type I had seen. They distorted his eyes and made them grotesque and hypnotic. Sometimes when he directed them at me with a giant frog's smile over an outsized bow tie, I felt as if a gigantic fish were leering at me through the glass of an aquarium and would be made to feel every bit of the dumb schoolboy that I was.

His method was too abstruse for me to absorb anything meaningful. It did spur me toward some good habits such as organizational techniques and odd bits of philosophy known to successful orchestrators like, "Good orchestrating is knowing what to leave out," "One string bass can carry a whole symphony orchestra," and "Write bottom up," which we come to once again and is such a seminal maxim; things like that.

Leafing through a few pages of Lange's "Study Notes" for those months rewarded me with a cascade of compositional truths:

- "...strong resolve vs. weak resolve..."
- "delayed resolutions ... landing place..."
- "...oblique motion vs. counterpoint..."
- charts and drawings of string bowing, double stop possibilities...
- bowing markings, facile inversions, harp pedalings and glissandos, various tempi indications, and now reference to more orchestral instruments, cadences, dependency, and independency.

One wonders what Spengler would have thought of Lange's conversion of the aural world into the "light-world." Nevertheless, it was an ingenious method for conceptualizing oral phenomena but a very abstract means when narrowed to an analysis of harmony—more like assigning colors to keys. This mind-blowing technology monopolized my efforts at a time when I should have been clutching Piston's basic book on *Harmony* to my bosom and never letting go.

Somehow all of the seemingly wasted childhood lessons, sporadic practice time, failed recitals, Brad Ormsby's ear and left-hand harmonic lessons, Murray Spivack's rhythm drills, Arthur Lange's incomprehensible Spectrotone, schoolmate jamming of simplistic jazz, gigs, and half-speed recordings, plus André Previn's inspiring role and my professional stint with Hoagy Carmichael, not to mention a welter of criticism, stories, and gossip added up to a very active musical life, though one not centered on piano.

Indirectly inspired by my custodial sessions with Oscar, I sought out a legendary Hollywood teacher, Sam Saxe. He was known chiefly as an improvisation coach, not only for piano, which was his basic instrument, but for other instrumentalists who wanted to improve their jazz ad-libbing ability. He lived in a tiny bungalow just three blocks from the TV studio on Vine Street where I worked. Very often I spent my lunch hour simply walking over and taking a piano lesson. The walls of his minute living room were covered with signed, framed photographs of all of his former students, some of them fairly well known. In the center of the cloistered room were crammed a broken-down grand piano, assorted functional and nonfunctional recording and playback devices, speakers, stack upon stack of music and manuscripts, and reams of blank manuscript paper.

Sam was another retreaded New Yorker. He, like Brad Ormsby, Murray Spivack, and Arthur Lange, had found his new life in the California sun where he could promote his system, in this case called—hold onto your seat—"The Sam Saxe System" (QED). It was not as complex as Lange's nor as simple as Ormsby's, but it was based on the same method that I had stumbled on for teaching myself to orchestrate. Sam's specialty was finding definitive examples of jazz piano styles—Bud Powell, Oscar Peterson, Thelonius Monk, and others, and slowing records down a full octave to half speed. Then he could copy off a note-for-note transcription of the artist's solo just as I had copied out orchestra parts. Some of these solos, such as Oscar Peterson's thirty-second-note runs, caused the piano music to look like one of Liszt's Opera Fantasies.

The idiosyncrasies of these independent teachers are probably worth a whole book by themselves. Sam would start each lesson by placing a sheet of clean manuscript paper on the music rack and carefully inscribing the words "Lesson Sheet" at the top of this page, followed by the student's name and the date. To accomplish this he used a calligraphic Esterbrook copy pen which imparted the artistic look of a Gothic monastery document with horizontal pen strokes being very wide and vertical strokes being very narrow.

Double-spaced below this header legend would be inscribed in one-half-inch block letters the work stages for the hour at hand. As the time progressed the student would see unfold before him the titles of all pieces worked on, metronome speeds, exercises, assignments for next time, and even a stray comment such as "...likes Charlie Mingus's...," all numbered and appearing like lines of the Ten Commandments. At the bottom, when the lesson was concluded, he would sign with a flourish, "Sam Saxe ... etc.," followed by his full address and telephone number. As far as I know every single lesson sheet, exercise, and page of transcribed manuscript, even those running to multiple pages, was signed individually by Sam. This reminded me of the old set of Shakespeare I bought once that bore an affectionate three-line inscription from a father to his daughter in all seventeen volumes with the same detailed avowal of love: help, Freud!

The student would commence a snail's-pace performance of the piece to a metronome's beat, much as one would normally do in learning difficult classical passages. At the end of the segment assigned he would write the new metronome setting achieved plus the date on the music in successive performances. Constant repetition eventually led to enough increase in speed to constitute a playable rendition of the artist's original improvisations. Sam would often reinforce the piece under study with an appropriate exercise pattern, also on a separate sheet, and *also* with metronome markings and dates, and *also* signed and addressed by himself. It was not a bad imitative technique.

Sam's method, as eccentric as parts of it seemed, embodied some basic principles that apply in one form or another to any well organized music study program. Even though his orientation was toward jazz improvisation, he respected fundamental scales and exercises, Hanon and Czerny types of drills if you will. He would adapt these for jazz work by indicating accents offbeat for a syncopated effect and always insisting that drills be done in all keys, ALL twelve keys and often the minors—all *three* minors. Often he had you attempt to play them in reverse or reframe them from eighth notes to triplets. He favored the metronome for developing rhythmic fidelity and for setting early goals. Sight-reading was a daily requirement for which you could utilize any old sheet music which he kept around for the purpose. He shoveled it out to his students in heaps, asking only that they return it after going through it once.

Sam managed to work in a few selections of classical music. Even for those wholly committed to jazz, he emphasized that no pianist's studies were complete without some exposure to the classics, a requirement which turned out fortuitously in my case. Subtly beginning with the last item of the lesson sheet, then expanding to the last two, there would begin to appear these assignments of the classic pieces of intermediate difficulty. More often than not they would include something by Chopin. I found myself enjoying the practice and memorization of some of these pieces that I had remembered less fondly from the dreaded days of grammar school classes and recitals. With some I seemed to relish playing them as much as I did thirty-two bars of tough Bud Powell. There was a lot of similarity. Sam tended to favor warhorses like "Malaguena" and "Ritual Fire Dance," but he would also sandwich in more durable and pleasant Chopin Waltzes, Impromptus, and Mazurkas. He would create columns showing recorded performances of numerous artists and qualify them as to "speed," "phrasing," "length," or "dynamic variation," and note any obvious stylistic characteristics like "Brings out sotto voce," "String quartet effect," or "Strict rhythm here." Though not by any means the mainstream of his training, I took great pleasure working on that little repertoire. All of those standards were learned as subsidiary pieces simply as adjuncts to the principal work on the jazz transcriptions. Even after I left Sam, I tried to maintain that fundamental repertoire.

Like the response in the old joke about the man in New York asking, "How do I get to Carnegie Hall?" being, "Practice! Practice! Practice," Sam repeated those words constantly, sometimes even writing them many times on the lesson sheet. There was something challenging and exhilarating about his boldly written goals that came at you like well-spaced hurdles which you jumped during the week. Any advance in speed and competence earned you a crisp new sheet with its daunting new hurdles.

Throughout the two years I was with Sam Saxe I watched him delicately alter my musical taste. I had started with Sam knowing little but the pop-jazz of the 1940s. This swing sound of the war years alternately amused and bored him. Mel Powell, Teddy Wilson, and Jess Stacy were pianists of the old era who had improvised chiefly around diatonic chords. Sam and his students were interested in the next generation of performers. He saw to it that I experienced some of the new music that was being created by Parker, Gillespie, Powell, Monk, and Davis in the 1950s, those who moved away from chordal resolutions on the dominant beats. Most of his other students were wildly enthusiastic about these artists.

Sam died several years ago, and so his marvelous signature is gone. His method survived with some of his senior students. The reason was, it was actually a valid system. It was a piece-by-piece, building-block approach to learning and an excellent technique for measuring progress on the way, whether in the jazz or classical arenas.

These mentors all preceded the trip to Paris and my pianistic epiphany, following which I had to go in search of someone who would lead the way. This business of going out into the current world and seeking the right teacher is as tricky as any commitment to a long-term relationship. It is not an easy task for any one of us and much more complicated for an amateur of middle age.

The teacher I found after my return from Paris was Robert Dick. Mr. Dick taught in his home much as Sam Saxe did. His piano was in better condition, and instead of one, he had two. In lieu of being surrounded by the cornice-high files of transcriptions, he was barricaded by the ubiquitous thick yellow albums of Schirmer, grey of Peters, blue of Henle, green of Kalmus and Ricordi, orange of Schott, and the cheap pictorial gloss of Dover: those formidable collected editions of two handfuls of familiar composers that comprise the torso of the body of traditional piano literature.

Robert Dick was an old-fashioned piano teacher who would have been comfortable in an antimacassared parlor with tiny candies in twisted wrappers standing in an epergne. He utilized tried and true conventional methods and did not set foot into the field of popular music and jazz improvisation. When David Copperfield's Aunt Betsey said, "Nobody knows what that man's mind is," she could easily have been talking about *this* Mr. Dick, the piano teacher. He seemed able to instruct pupils of any age and even taught other teachers, which is no mean feat.

Mr. Dick had suffered two heart attacks but was amazingly strong and giving of himself, despite these setbacks. He was slightly hard of hearing after a lifetime dose of amateur performances, a fact that endowed him with a Christian willingness to forgive mistakes. Piano music and music in general had been his life. He had much to impart. Sometimes just talking with him would help a student surmount a problem or pull a piece together. Many of the tricks covered in the chapter on practicing are some of his repeated technical antidotes.

It seems simple to remind oneself that steady rhythm is important, or that one should breathe between phrases and really feel their separation, or be watchful in bringing out inner voices, or any one of a dozen or so Golden Rules with which every pianist is familiar. Since we cannot all do all things at all times, the value of a Mr. Dick was to help his students select and emphasize just those elements of practice to which he could give the highest priorities.

The legendary Mr. Dick of Dickens's invention was able to resolve David Copperfield's terrified vision of the future when he uttered the simple words, "Have him measured for a suit of clothes directly." So too, our Mr. Dick preached these sacred problem-solving pronouncements. They are worth chiseling on a tablet of stone to stand in perpetuity:

- Beat two silent measures (to establish rhythm).
- Select an easy, realistic tempo (not strained).
- Keep a steady rhythm.(!!!)
- Think from the bottom up (building from the bass).(!!!)
- Breathe deeply.(!!)
- Keep your eyes on the page, not the keyboard.
- Produce the dynamics indicated.(!!)
- Phrase logically, like sentences.(!!)
- Be artistic and aesthetic. Make music.(!!!)
- Do not use too much pedal.

Any way you look at it, short of the psychiatrist's couch, the piano teacher remains as one of the last exciting and legitimate bastions of the old-world personal tutor. Consider the cost of a college education for even one year, versus the individuality available from a devoted and gifted piano teacher.

Chapter 4

How to Judge a Piano

In this age of computers, VCRs, CDs, and DATs, it is small wonder that we have become accustomed to high prices combined with speedy obsolescence. Fashion and model changes plus electronic innovation rapidly age the products we own. Charges for repairs rival those of replacement. Often parts are no longer available. We are constantly being urged to replace old goods with new ones, which usually forces us to discard or sell off the quickly antiquated ones at a fraction of their initial cost. A well-chosen piano is an exception.

However, the world is full of bad pianos. Most of these are the broken down, neglected relics that lurk in our homes, apartments, and schoolrooms like spavined nags. Others crowd the piano stores of our nation. Still others skulk in our auditoriums and halls masquerading as serious concert grands and feigning a look of tuxedoed elegance when their interiors are as rickety and diseased as carcasses on a garbage dump. The United States is engorged with terrible pianos.

Vic Braden, at the initial session of his tennis clinics is invariably asked by one of the class members, "Mr. Braden, which racket would you recommend?" His cynically comic answer is, "It doesn't make any difference. The worst one of them is better than the best one of you."

Tough but funny? Yes, when applied to tennis rackets, and probably true. No, when applied to pianos where it is a case of needing the best. That is to say, the best you can afford and can accommodate.

In order to make this musical commitment truly fun and worthwhile, you want to seek out a fine, well-maintained instrument. If you have a piano and it is in good condition you may face only the necessity of periodic tuning *and*, of course, *voicing*, about which there is more to say later. If your piano is in poor shape but can be made pleasurable by regulating the action, replacing the hammers, overhauling the action, or even restringing, it may be worth doing as long as you have the advice of a professional. As a general rule, old pianos are seldom worth totally restoring at prices you must pay for this work except for certain models of Steinway or very special models of a few other brands that also retain strong resale market value.

Fortunately, a well-chosen, well-bought piano, whether new or used, will generally retain its value. Due to the constant escalation of labor rates, the fact that a piano is a labor intensive creation causes the products of good quality to appreciate as time goes on.

New Pianos

Yamaha	Steinway (New York)
Kimball	Steinway (Hamburg)
Baldwin	Bösendorfer
Mason & Hamlin	Bechstein
Schimmel	Blüthner
I Chang	Grotrian
Sammick	Ibach
Kawai	Feurich
Falcone	

In terms of sheer numbers produced, Yamaha, Kimball, and Kawai are light-years ahead of the pack. They employ mass production and marketing methods that spawn pianos in the hundreds of thousands. The materials used and the hard, mirrorlike finishes are comparable in design and appearance to the reliable European makes. Fine woods and real ivory keys are available. By maintaining this large volume and a high degree of automation, their prices are kept competitive. With attention and care applied over the years, there is no reason why a better quality U.S. or Japanese product should not provide long life and adequate resale potential.

On the other hand, though more costly to begin with, the low output of American Steinway, the tiny Falcone company, and the leading European brands offer an opportunity to associate oneself with one of the truly worthwhile possessions of a lifetime. These pianos are predominantly hand made and become more rare as the years go by.

The golden age of modern pianoforte-making lay between the two world wars, basically in the 1920s. Many cities and towns in

Europe had their own small piano factories where a nucleus of highly skilled workers and a treasure trove of painstakingly selected and preserved woods lay in readiness, to be assembled ultimately into works of art.

Following the devastation of World War II, the number of small regional factories shrank to a handful. Fortunately there remained enough trained technicians to enable some of those left to consolidate into viable postwar businesses and perpetuate these workers' skills. In Europe, therefore, there exist several top manufacturers such as Steinway, Bösendorfer, Bechstein, Blüthner, and Grotrian. This continuity of concept, design, and artisan skills had considerably less momentum in the United States. The early promise of such enterprising companies as Chickering, Mason & Hamlin, and Baldwin was overshadowed by American Steinway, which for many years has been the dominant prestige piano manufacturer.

The Steinway produces a bold, frontal attack on its listeners that makes it a formidable instrument for public performance and when played in ensemble work with an orchestra. It performs gladiatorially in large halls. In competitions where young pianists from around the globe are offered a choice of many instruments, there are few who take the risk of playing anything other than the American Steinway.

Steinway now has new private owners. This group has vowed to change whatever negative image existed. The present plan has been to utilize a greater number of superior German parts in the domestic U.S. actions, presumably combining the finest components of manufacturers on each side of the Atlantic. Along with this they claim to be concentrating on quality control, both at the factory and through reorganization of their dealer network, with a firm eye on justifying their position of leadership. Most important of all, sales have been keeping up well with supplies. In fact, in some markets there is even a waiting list for certain models, at this writing at least.

European Pianos

The pure, round, more subtle tone of European pianos has long been a fond obsession of mine. Asian and U.S. pianos seem exceedingly bright and often harsh by comparison and often sometimes less well made, being mass-produced units.

There is a prevalent thought that you should acquire the largest and finest instrument possible. It can be overdone, of course. Keep in mind that one needs the freedom to perform and practice with abandon. The neighbors aside, a gigantic piano in a confined space is inhibiting and can even be painful and harmful to the ears. It is sad that the U.S. manufacturers have abandoned the nice 6′ plus "A" size, sometimes called a "Drawing Room Model." It is still available in foreign imports and enjoys the type of bass string length capable of producing an adequate, satisfying tone. So, too, we have been deprived of the 7′5″ "C" size, called the Parlor Concert Grand, also still made in Europe and Japan. This is excellent for a large room or small hall without the dominant, rumbling bass of the 9′ standard concert grand. Both the "A" and "C" sizes have good "scaling," by which is meant the transitions among the various string diameters that can sometimes display jarringly unmatched tonal qualities as one progresses from one part of the piano to another.

In the absence of the "A" or "C," universally the 6′ 10½″ "B" size is looked upon as the most satisfactory for the professional or dedicated amateur for all-around use and day-to-day practice. It is best to stay above 6′ to avoid weak bass strings, though there is the occasional gem scattered here and there around the globe, but who would want to sell it? And what buyer would present himself at the exact moment such a rarity was offered?

The *tone* of pianos is an important and highly subjective matter. Public performance, conditions, mass marketing, public-relations-artist contracts, modern stereo systems in homes, movie theatres, and auditoriums, plus altered public taste — not to mention modern factory production methods — have all had their effect on the way pianos sound. In hundreds of thousands of pianos being fabricated today, the emphasis seems to be for instant brilliance in tone production. A mass producer would be foolhardy to fly in the face of this brash metallic sound that every purchaser, competitor, and media representative seems to desire.

Almost all new pianos — particularly American and Asian — possess this keen brilliance. Complaining about this is like objecting to the sound of excessive high frequencies in the majority of stereo speakers. The lamentable fact is that the public has been trained to associate that forced sibilance with a phoney "liveness."

In the salons of Europe it was generally the case during the "Golden Age" of piano making, between the two world wars, that

Hamburg Steinways, Bechsteins, Blüthners, and Bösendorfers were supplied with hand-felted hammers lovingly created with skill and care by patient craftsmen. The gentle, yielding crowns of the early hammers coaxed warm, honeyed tones from the depths of those instruments. Bass notes did not merge with one another. One could assume that years of gentle playing would steadfastly bring about a gradual increased brilliance as the felt compacted over time, just as years of cellaring can delicately age a fine wine.

We must, however, awaken to the current age. Now our Renner-type hammers start their life in a hardened, compressed condition. Felt is literally mashed onto the wooden core of the hammers by pressing devices that can doubtless crank out thousands in a day. The resultant hammers become little weapons as hard as xylophone mallets. For the buyer with a sensitive ear it can take a technician a full working day of difficult, painstaking labor to soften and voice these ball peen mallets by needling them one by one to restore the felt's resilience.

Those who are alert to fine piano craftsmanship can take heart from the fact that there is still a high level of materials and quality handwork incorporated in the new instruments made by several of the fine old companies. Custom casework and other cosmetics are generally superb. Handmade, old-fashioned soft, rounded hammers can still be purchased from certain specialty manufacturers. Seasoned lumber from trees just a specific number of feet from their native river and sometimes ivory from the endangered elephant are still around. The quest is not hopeless. That fine sound of a truly musical piano is still obtainable.

In the European tradition, the *Hamburg Steinway* used to be an easier playing piano, also producing a sweeter, more musical tone than its U.S. brother. Graham Reed, in an informative series of articles in *The Piano Quarterly* in 1987, points out that it is now noted for a more aggressive sound. Of the various pianos made in Europe, the Hamburg Steinway usually commands the highest price.

It is hard not to mention *Bösendorfer* in the same breath. This Viennese-made piano is still fabricated with a case that comes from a single core of spruce. This method is unlike all of its competitors', who use bent, laminated sheets of plywood to form the outer sides of the piano. It possesses other design features, such as the added keys, that provide increased range on the larger instruments. The tone of the modern Bösendorfer is brilliant without being harsh or strident, rather silvery in color. Bass notes have a singular, slightly hollow voice that is distinct and unique. They express a proud sonority, and not often mentioned is a delightful, cushion-like feel to the keybed. A Bösendorfer is an ideal medium for music of the baroque and classic periods and, interestingly enough, jazz. Moreover, this company enjoys a reputation as the one most devoted to factory predelivery preparation. The precise fitting of tuning pins and pin block assures an unusual longevity to its periodic tunings. The price of the Bösendorfer is quite near that of the Hamburg Steinway.

Bechstein of Berlin set the standard of the industry in Europe and the world for many years. To this day it is an instrument of very fine quality, though its tone can lean a bit to the thin side. However, in the hands of a sensitive pianist the mid-bass possesses an uncanny ability to sound as if a cello has taken the place of your fingers. As Reed says, "the action responsiveness is a true marvel and can reveal all manner of subtleties the player never knew he could produce." No piano can execute the gauzy meanderings of impressionist composers better than the Bechstein. It stands for the pinnacle of gracious living as a cornerstone of sophisticated parlor performances. Casework and finishing touches are exemplary. Its price is slightly less than that of Steinway and Bösendorfer.

The less well-known *Blüthner* is made in Leipzig behind what used to be the Iron Curtain. Soviet officials seemed determined to keep this revered product competitive with the best pianos of the Western world. Blüthner installs actions that are comparable in quality to the other makers', though there can be some variation from piano to piano as is always the case. Check your fast repeated trills, and tonal evenness with great care.

Tone is everything here. A mid-range note sounded on a Blüthner actually *grows* or "blooms" after the initial striking. The "Aliquot" or extra overtone strings may contribute to this, but the results are undeniable. Reed correctly states that a Blüthner "just will not produce an ugly tone." Prices are reasonable at the time of writing for these lovely pianos, due chiefly to a depressed East German economy. Even with a 40 percent duty on new instruments coming in through U.S. customs (as opposed to 6 percent for West European pianos), their reputation for sweet, mellow sound can offer a fine addition to any domestic environment. With the political changes in the now defunct East Germany, the duty may be lowered. If ever you yearned to hear the "yang and yin" of bass note sound, you should contrive to hear this comparison on a Blüthner and a Bösendorfer. There could be no clearer enunciation of two opposed concepts of tonal production, both with their own unique appeal.

Grotrian, Feurich, Schimmel, Ibach, Forrester, and others are also manufactured in small quantities to very high standards and at somewhat lower cost.

In the United States the listed price of imported pianos seems unwarrantedly high. One reason is the small quantity that are imported. Another is the difficulty of selling any instrument over $20,000. This seems to be the price level of the psychological "break point." Inasmuch as a dealer may be stuck with one or more of these European pianos on his showroom floor literally for years, he must build the interest on that committed capital and overhead into his asking price in the hope of one day bailing out and realizing a profit. However, there is no law against your proposing to make a fair offer and seeing what develops.

Asian and U.S. Pianos

As for the two major *Japanese brands* of Kawai and Yamaha, it can be said that they represent a fine value for the money. The Kawai R1A, in particular, is hand made in the manner of the European instruments, and with respect to elegance of execution should almost be compared with them. It is a heavy, extremely solid, elegant piece of work. The action on the one I tried was a little stiff but would presumably become more responsive with regulation and the passage of time. The tone was full and even throughout the keyboard. However, despite all that is good about these brands, I simply have a predilection for European pianos, which may go all the way back to the provenance of the compositions that are generally played on them.

No discussion of American pianos would be complete these days without mentioning Santi Falcone. He has originated his own U.S. piano factory near Boston. He wisely turns out three sizes: the 6' 1" Conservatory size, the 7' 4" C or small concert, and, of course, the 9' Concert Grand. These pianos are very well made, reasonably priced, and sound a bit like the Hamburg Steinway, having the slightly sweeter and more musical sound of the European instruments.

Falcone, being a good entrepreneur, has managed to place a few of his instruments around in various symphonies and institutions that count. He is having luck with some artists whose contracts permit their using something besides Steinways in concert or in chamber work. Bravo, Santi! Buona fortuna!

The two Golden Ages of the American Steinway were between the two world wars, the era that built its reputation, and during the 1950s. This would be prior to the CBS takeover of the company and naturally prior to the introduction of teflon bushings. Moreover, that period is supposed to represent a culmination in design, craftsmanship, and materials to produce a very special piano. That is often why a well-preserved instrument of that period in the meaningful B or D sizes is eagerly sought after and generally commands a premium price on the used piano market.

Along with the passing of so many niceties of the past, we must shed a tear for the demise of ivory keys. They are now a thing of the past. Not only the United States, but all Common Market countries have outlawed the use of elephant tusks for commercial purposes. Except for used pianos and rare black-market adventures, the precious material that was said to cushion the fingers and absorb perspiration has vanished from the scene.

The *finish* of a piano had best be black. Perhaps it is a coincidence or a prejudice—I am not sure which—but I cannot recall ever having played a piano in natural hardwood that had exceptional tone. There must be exceptions. I cannot attest to the qualities of all-white pianos because I have forbidden myself ever to play one. They belong in shipboard movies of the 1940s or in Noel Coward plays.

The science of piano manufacture is competitive, mercurial and flawed. The critical judgment of the players, audience, and critics is prejudiced and subjective. The quality of instruments from the same manufacturers can vary greatly due to materials, conditions, workmanship, and probably such variables as schedules, worker turnover, sick leaves, vacations, coffee breaks, moods, humors, and, oh yes, luck. I even harbor the cynical picture of the president of the factory—as surely the Signori Stradivarius, Guarnerius, and Amati must have done with their violins—when he gets wind of a superior piano in the workroom, simply setting it aside for his own use or telling his favorite artist about it. Wouldn't you, if you owned the factory? Yet out of this welter of confusion we nevertheless must form some guidelines for selection and commitment to an instrument.

Maybe the time has come to admit that there *is* a grain of truth in Vic Braden's callous dig at the tennis player's ability measured against his equipment. The big variable, after all, is in ourselves. Given a certain functional minimum it may be that beautiful, soulful music can be wrung out of any reasonable assemblage of wires and hammers once we adopt an existential stance that the music is us and the piano a mere extension of our art.

This is not to demote the elaborate and thrilling prospect of acquiring, reshaping, and enjoying the best instrument possible. It is merely to state that there comes a time when we must get on with it and begin playing. Tolstoy's short story "How Much Land a Man Needs," if it were retitled "How Much Can a Person Analyze a Piano?" might aptly suggest the self-indulgence implicit in this negative exercise of over-preparedness. More fruitful might be a discipline of negatives whereby you concentrate on what you *don't* want in a piano. In any event, it is time to get on with it.

Purchasing a Piano

The Best. Who would not like to own a concert grand? What piano enthusiast's eyes do not light up nor pulse quicken at the sight of a 9′ black beauty? Who indeed? A little squib in *The New Yorker* captured the ecstasy of this moment so precisely when it described a woman this way: "The look that came into her eyes as she passed the kitchen door revealing the professional ranges, salamander, deep stainless sinks, warming drawers, baking ovens, gleaming copper pots on endless racks and gigantic stock pots and ladles was like that of a pianist who unexpectedly catches sight of a glamorous concert grand."

Verticals. These space-saving and money-saving instruments come in four basic styles that vary chiefly with respect to their heights. Spinets go up to 40″; Consoles up to 43″; Studios up to 47″; and Full Uprights up to 60″. The action and tone are generally inferior to grands'. Still, when space or budget dictates this type of unit, it is comforting to know that there are some decent products on the market. The English Welmar is quite a nice little piano, particularly in the "A" series. Knight is another. Also all of the prestigious makers offer vertical pianos, but these are quite expensive and would certainly rival the price of a used grand in good condition.

Used Pianos. We stated at the outset that a very high percentage, in fact almost all pianos, are improperly maintained and in abysmal condition. Generally they are neither tuned, cleaned, voiced, regulated, closed when not in use, protected from maids, drinkers, cats, vases, bric-a-brac, sharp picture frames, nor treated lovingly. Under these assumed conditions they cannot help but fester and deteriorate. In the hands of an expert technician and restorer they can be brought back to acceptability, or even be completely restored. However, this latter option is an expensive, time consuming and imperfect undertaking that is fraught with numerous potentials for failure, not the least of which is a likely loss of capital.

Despite these dire words of cynicism, a patient probing of the "Pianos for Sale" by private parties in the classified section of your Sunday newspaper is eminently worthwhile. Being admitted to heaven could be no less rapturous than the event of stumbling across a choice instrument that combines: (1) a single long-term owner; (2) a legitimate motivation for selling; (3) evidence of tender loving care; and (4) softness of price.

It is impracticable to haul a technician around to inspect every crate of wire, screws, and hammers that comes your way. Larry Fine's excellent book on piano buying will tell you everything you need to know on this subject. Some current pricing needs to be adjusted since the market prices change mercurially. Also I would give more space to some of the prestigious European imports. Still, it is highly recommended for this purpose.

These are a few cursory examinations a layman can and should make. Here are some rules to keep in mind.

• Pianos are basically hard to sell. Unlike cars and russet potatoes they are not a necessity. Thus, there is usually a perpetual buyer's market. Possibly excepting the larger Steinways made after 1920, prices tend to be soft, often very soft.

• Pianos are excruciatingly hard for an owner to sell out of his home. This makes the classified ads of large Sunday papers a happy hunting ground for bargain-minded buyers.

• Favor grands over vertical pianos because of their superior tone and better action, providing that space and budget are flexible.

• Strive for a length in excess of six feet in order to achieve a proper length of bass strings.

• Shop only for a black piano, as with tuxedos, dress shoes, and turtle-necked sweaters (if you admire Ned Rorem).
Sellers seek an unwarranted premium for natural finished pianos, probably because they cost more initially.

When it comes right down to inspecting an instrument, here are some suggestions:

• Listen for an even, resonant tone from *top to bottom* of the keyboard, particularly in the "killer octaves" that represent the highest two and one-half octaves. Beware of thinness or nasality of tone. Test by playing slow arpeggios from the bass up into the treble and by being alert to this desired evenness of tone and volume. Compare the natural resonance of the lower notes to a convincing sustained quality of the uppers.

• Strive for a singing treble and mid-treble. Simply sound individual notes of the top two and one-half octaves in descending order and back up again. Do they sing? If you have a sweep second-hand on your watch, time the "decay" or dying out of a struck note in the top two octaves. Evidence of decay in less than four seconds should be cause for terminating the examination. Few pianos pass this test.

• Test for a responsive, easy-to-play action. It shouldn't be so light that your fingers seem to fly off your hands. It needs to react instantaneously to your applied finger pressure *and* to the rapid repetition of the same note plus trills. Test with Schubert's Opus 90, No. 4, one of the best for this. Chopin's Scherzo in B-flat minor, second theme, has some repeated notes that are ideal for this test. So, too, are the ornaments in the first measure of Bach's B-flat Partita, and Haydn's Sonata in G.

• Determine if the keybed has a comfortable feeling, not too cushioned nor hard as bedrock.

• Articulate keys up and down, then sideways to check for clicks indicating sloppy action, malfunctioning knuckles, or loose key bushings.

• Check hammers for deep key grooving, excessive compaction, or recent filing. These grooves and dents are obvious and easily removed by filing and reshaping as long as there is enough felt remaining.

• Depress a cluster of contiguous keys slowly, holding them

down just to the point where the hammers return to the underneath side of the strings. Note whether they are in an even line. Failure to reposition themselves in an even "after-touch" position means that the action will require regulation.

• Strike notes systematically and release them with a specific ear to whether the dampers are doing their job. If you hear any lingering overtones the dampers are not seating completely.

• Evaluate the cosmetic condition of the case, fall board, music rack, strings, pedals, and hardware. Determine if the piano has been refinished. Lots of clues are there to help you with this, such as gilt paint not being applied between and under the strings and the orange-peel look of sprayed-on paint such as you might see in a fresh car paint job that had not been rubbed out. Check the originality of felts woven through the strings and in numerous places of trim throughout the piano.

• Sight the bottom of the soundboard. Look for cracks and con- cavities. Place a bright light above or below the board to check for fissures. Try to stretch a length of string as far as you can along the flat underneath of the soundboard to see if you can detect the crown of the soundboard, which should be about one-quarter inch.

• If the piano is in a damp part of the country, check for rust. Has the owner used a "heat stick" or "damp chaser?" Are the strings rusty? Rub them with your pocket handkerchief and you will know soon enough.

• Evaluate the degree of overall cleanliness, especially of felts and keys.

• Throughout the mid-bass to bass range test the clarity of triads and simple major sevenths, that is a two-note chord of, say, a C and the B-natural eleven notes above it. European pianos generally show to advantage when comparing these lower chords, with the American Steinway often responding with a threatening canine growl. This defi- ciency is usually offset by upper-end brilliance: you must judge.

Since you may be examining a variety of instruments you can undertake the analysis up to this point on your own. Then when you reach a serious offering stage with any piano seek the help of a good technician or a member of the Piano Technicians Guild.

A form such as that used by many technicians is included in the Appendix. While there are too many confusing categories incor- porated in it for the layman's understanding, it should be helpful in making you aware of what is involved in a comprehensive evaluation.

Chapter 5

The Library of Music

One of the great pleasures of life can be the acquisition of lovely things, particularly if they last a long time and don't cost too much. Buying a library of music fits this description to a "t."

As a bible is to a church, navigational charts to a boat, and a script to a play, your library of music is a set of maps for the exploration of the piano. Besides the library's seminal role in your musical life, it remains a constant joy even to contemplate because it means that any standard work is readily available for silent reading, practice, or performance. Furthermore, it functions as an invaluable set of reference works, able to give a lifetime of pleasure without needing to be updated. Whenever you have the urge to study a piece merely by reading it over—and how many artists recommend this before starting work at the piano!—or while listening to a recording to check tempi and phrasing, there neatly cased by your piano resides the perfect foundation for all that can follow.

Considerable pleasure can be had in deliberating about and acquiring the various albums and pieces of music in the library. The purpose in this chapter is to provide you with some tools, or at least opinions, to assist in selecting the richest assortment of music available.

Good music is still being published worldwide, though retail stores selling it in this country have been decreasing in number due to the specialized nature of the product. Rental costs for downtown retail space have skyrocketed, many older merchants of long standing have died or retired, and slow turnover of the product all account for some of this shrinkage in retail outlets. Moreover, U.S. publishers, particularly Schirmer which was at one time the major source, seem to undergo frequent reorganization and change in sales and distribution patterns, further frustrating our search for dependable, vital sources.

Luckily some stores in a few major cities and some outlets of publishers still do carry quite complete lines of publications and most offer them by mail. Information about these essential suppliers can be found later in this chapter. The very catalogues of the major publishers provide a juicy fund of knowledge for the development of your library, and music is very fairly priced and often much cheaper than books that you read once and put on the shelf. When you consider the length of the pleasure it can provide—years!—and the quality of that pleasure, it's a bargain.

I am enraptured by the things William S. Newman has to say on the importance of forming a music library in his book, *The Pianist's Problems:*

> [T]he basic library furnishes a prime means of cultivating musicianship, just as it furnishes a fund of literature from which the pianist can draw pieces he studies to perform. . . . As soon as the student shows promise of continuing interest, he should (buy) in one lump purchase those works that represent the cornerstones of piano literature—those works that would be essential to his musical pleasure were he to be stranded on a desert isle.

In other words, go for it. Not too fast, though, because there is a lot of fun available in the planning, picking and choosing, and ultimate buying. I would suggest setting out a program for assembling your ideal piano music library.

Newman points out several advantages to this library assemblage:

• The student supplies himself at once with resources constantly at hand for future exploration, study, and beneficial enjoyment. They are basic.

• Volumes are always cheaper, by a long shot, than the sum of individual pieces; also, albums are sometimes on sale; seldom, single copies.

• A rounded library is protection against gaps in the student's repertoire.

• This basic library helps guard against unbalanced tastes, such as a passion for Bartók and an aversion to Chopin!

Don't overlook used music or libraries of music you occasionally find for sale. Newman does caution against the tendency toward pure or *Urtext* editions. The barren notation of these cleansed editions can produce confusion for the amateur who might not have sufficient experience with Bach, for example, to tackle him with virtually no editorial markings, no help on ornamentation, etc.

Just as in the selection of the piano itself and the books we choose to read, there should be discrimination applied to assembling a fine library of music. There exist volumes of music that are more attractive than others, that have superior scholarship, more pleasing format, clearer notation, better fingering, are more imaginative and instructive, and—in the case of Donald Tovey—have livelier, wittier comments. Welcome and relish the job of collecting a dynamic library, not simply by purchasing the most widely distributed and most easily accessible material from the local music store, but by ordering music on a very selective basis from a wealth of worldwide sources. Bless these publishers and be thankful they still exist, for having a piano covered only with canary yellow G. Schirmer albums is like having the living room coffee table monopolized by the *National Geographic*. There are often more enlightened choices that could be made.

Cloth-bound volumes of music obviously cost more than paper. Moreover, they frequently have to be ordered since few dealers carry much variety in stock. However, the standard, oft-repeated works like Bach's "Well-Tempered Clavier" and Inventions, Chopin's Sonatas, Etudes, Preludes, Nocturnes, and Polonaises are relied upon to such an extent throughout a pianist's life that it is false economy not to include them in the library in the most permanent of reference forms, which is in durable, toughly sewn, heavy backed, cloth bindings.

Also, it is the nature of a large, cloth-covered book with hard covers, once broken in, to lie back against the music rack in docile repose and permit its pages to be turned effortlessly and permanently without the vexation of constantly having to flex the spine of softer material or seeing your play interrupted to flip back previously turned pages as though they were unruly locks of hair. Maintaining your own equanimity as a player demands that a turned page lie calmly as a lovingly trained spaniel and not insinuate itself again with persistent aggression.

These are commonly available cloth-bound editions:

Composer	Henle	Peters	Assoc. Board
Bach	Most all	Most all	Most all
Beethoven	Sonatas	Sonatas	Sonatas
	Variations	Sonatas*	
Brahms	Misc. (2 vol.)		
Chopin	Most all	Most all	Most all
Haydn	Sonatas	Sonatas	Sonatas
	Variations		
Mendelssohn	Songs w/o Words	S w/o W	S w/o W
Mozart	Sonatas	Sonatas	Sonatas
	Misc. Pieces		
	Variations		
	Duets		
Schubert	Sonatas	Sonatas	
	Imp. and Mom. Mus.	I & MM	I & MM
Schumann	Works (3 vols.)	Works	

---

* Pocket-sized edition (for study)

With most popular novels costing between $15 and $25, these handsome, useful volumes are tremendous bargains at prices that run just a little more than that. Moreover, when we consider that they can provide a lifetime of enjoyment of study, enrichment, even solace, they would seem to be cheap at twice the price.

The Bibles. Professor Newman writes in his introduction to an early C. F. Peters Co. *Urtext* catalogue that the most frequently published works in numerous editions are—probably in order of popularity—Bach's Inventions (two-part) and Symphonia (three-part), Beethoven's Sonatas, Mozart's Sonatas, and Chopin's Nocturnes (QED). The basic reasons for continuing to publish their endless editions for over two centuries he submits to be:

- The role of the editor changes from era to era.
- There are changes in historical style.
- New facts about original material or sources become available.
- A desire for more authenticity develops.
- Notation is modernized.
- Editors have been constantly searching for an ever more "faithful" text.

It is often instructive and scintillating to have two or more editions of the same work available for cross-referencing notation (not notes, of course, but note values, stem direction, and how interpretation of hand placement might be viewed), fingering (wildly divergent sometimes), dynamics, phrasing, and, naturally, interpretative comments. Also, practicing a piece can sometimes be stimulated by approaching it by means of an alternative text.

There are also "study editions" that are available by artists like Schnabel (Beethoven), Cortot (Chopin, Liszt, Mendelssohn, Schubert, and Schumann), and others. These editions give you a healthy workout turning pages, inasmuch as the critical comments in most of them fill a substantial part of the pages. Nevertheless, they are invaluable as instructive guides.

Early Music. The one other dominant composer whose dates coincide roughly with Bach's—both were born in 1685—was Domenico Scarlatti. His hundreds of Sonatas are published in their entirety in a magnificent Thanksgiving-feast of an edition by Recordi, the Longo edition, named for his principal biographer and cataloger; much akin to what Köchel was for Mozart. This has been reprinted successfully by Edwin F. Kalmus Publishing at a considerably lower price. Selective editions of groups of the more popular sonatas are marketed by various publishers such as Peters and Schirmer. A choice number of his Sonatas was edited by Ruth Slenczynska and published by Stipes Publishing Company, and is exceedingly well chosen and well notated with her interpreted, sophisticated markings printed in a judicious red type that distinguishes them from the original text. The Associated Board also has a good selection of thirty-seven Sonatas that are graded as to level of play.

Bach. Most critics of Bach editions single out the Hans Bischoff complete works that are reproduced by Edwin F. Kalmus as most worthy. The volumes of this composer that should be in any serious pianist's library are the forty-eight Preludes and Fugues of the "Well-Tempered Clavier," Books 1 and 2, and the Two- and Three-Part Inventions (Sinfonia). I am fond of those published by the Associated Board and distributed in the United States by the Oxford University Press.

These volumes, whose printed notation is a bit old-fashioned, embody Donald Tovey's lengthy and comprehensive interpretive comments on each one of the pieces. This austere notation might find us wishing for a backup set of these seminal works, such as a Peters or Henle. Nevertheless, if you have room for only one set, *this* is the one to have.

In addition to the Preludes and Fugues, these are the other mandatory Bach albums:

	Recommended Edition
Inventions and Sinfonia	Henle or Peters
French and English Suites, Partitas	Henle or Peters
Toccatas	Henle or Peters
Chromatic Fantasie and Fugue, Italian Concerto, Prel. and Fugue in A minor	Schirmer

One can also order from C. F. Peters the Marcello Concerto transcribed for solo keyboard. It is not difficult and provides an opportunity to study and perform a short, delightful work of Bach's that is seldom heard.

Beethoven. All the world publishes these Sonatas. They are beautifully presented in two volumes by Henle with a good text, wide spacing, and clear notation which almost always characterizes these fine editions; also with an airy format whose only disadvantage lies in a need for fairly frequent turning of pages. This is caviling to be sure.

The Associated Board edition is presented in three volumes and also has the invaluable comments of Donald Tovey, as in the case of the "Well-Tempered Clavier." Once again, if the library is to contain only one edition, this is the one to have. These are older plates and the musical notation is a bit antiquated. Still, the prose is first class. Tovey's comments are helpful and amusing. They would be worth reading even if one were not a pianist. Incidentally, owning Tovey's *A Companion to Beethoven's Pianoforte Sonatas* does not take the place of the album notes. It covers different territory, being directed toward analysis rather than performance.

Writing of the 31st Sonata in A-flat Major, Opus 110, Tovey says,

> [I]t is no use deferring the study of such music until you feel ripe for it. Those who think it unimpressive are beyond the reach of advice. Those who recognize that they are not ready for it must remember that experience cannot come except by experience; . . . no criticism is so mean and mischievous as that which discourages . . . because "correctness is not enough." Who supposes that it is? . . .

[B]e able to think of the music without thinking of yourself; . . .
then receive more of Beethoven's message than you thought you
knew.

Schnabel's edition and comments are always worthwhile, considering the lineage that exists from Schnabel back to Busoni and
back to the master. The fingering is sometimes quirky but always
thought provoking.

Peters's newer edition is edited by Claudio Arrau and is very
good, as is their older one. Henle and Schirmer both have excellent
editions. There is a lot to choose from here.

The Thirty-Two Variations in C minor can be obtained
separately in a comely edition from Henle, also the Diabelli Variations and the Bagatelles. As a general rule you will find notes
squeezed closer together in Edwin F. Kalmus and Schirmer editions,
with the obvious good news being that you can economize on turning pages. It may cause a little eye squinting in the early learning
stages, but later, when the music becomes imprinted even partially
on the subconscious you find yourself thankful for fewer pages to
turn.

A warning about Edwin F. Kalmus: always be on your guard for
stapled or single-stitched volumes that won't stay open no matter
what you do, including major foot stomping.

Brahms. The easiest and best answer here is to buy the three-
volume set from Schirmer or the two-volume set from Henle or
Peters. Separate performing editions are also available. Like
Schumann, they are well worth having in both album and in the individual group form in the case of Opus Nos. 76, 117, 118, 119, and
the Paganini and Handel variations. The brief nature of most of
Brahms's piano compositions suggests buying all of his works and be
done with it. These are nuggets beyond praise, and the second
Schirmer book contains the prize collection of them all.

Chopin. Serious new contenders for the best issue of Chopin's
works would appear to be the Chopin Institute's "Paderewski" edition with its intriguing foreign-looking covers. They are well for-
matted and well printed. However, the Institute has utilized a
peculiar pulpy sort of paper, on which the likes of "Big-Little" books,

comic books, and wartime novels used to be printed, that makes for rapid deterioration on the turning corners. Some of the bindings are slipshod, causing the quires to part company after awhile. The headings of the individual pieces seem done by a cryptographer who was bent on concealing the end of one selection and the start of another. To which end he selected numbers from a Lilliputian font and chose to avoid the wide top margins that have come to signify the separations between multiple works. It is a good edition, nonetheless.

Be on guard also against albums which leave out the posthumous works, whether due to purity, penuriousness, or carelessness. Some publishers leave out the last three Waltzes and the last three posthumous Etudes, perhaps hoping thereby to beef up demand for their separate album of miscellaneous selections.

Though perhaps spurious as authentic Etudes, the first of these in F minor is worthy without doubt, and is said to have been requested by Liszt on his deathbed. Such transparent omissions should only whet your cunning, and speed you to a good decision unless you *want* the miscellaneous album.

Any serious amateur heeds *all* of the principal works of Chopin. You wouldn't get copies of *David Copperfield*, *A Tale of Two Cities*, and the Christmas stories, and feel that you had covered the bases as far as Dickens was concerned, surely. Same thing. No need to enumerate them. Just do it.

A special note is in order for the Etudes. The older French publication put out by Salabert and edited by Alfred Cortot is a bit like Tovey's treatment of the "Well-Tempered Clavier" and the Beethoven Sonatas without witty remarks. You can buy this edition in French or English. Once again, we are dealing with old-fashioned notation as with the Associated Board. That shouldn't make any difference. If it does, back it up with any good alternate edition.

The main objectives in the Cortot are the marvelous fingering, very thoroughly marked, and extensive supportive exercises on the beginning pages of *each* Etude. The fingering is imaginative and generously repeated in later duplicated figures, which is a rarity. Accents are found in uncommon but musically innovative and correct places.

To demonstrate, here are accents compared in Chopin's Etude, Opus 10, No. 4–Coda:

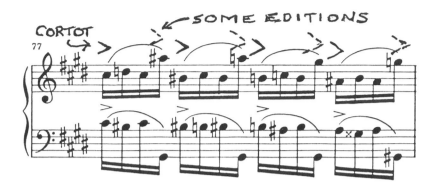

There is no doubt in my mind that Cortot's placement is more realistic and pianistic.

Cortot editions are handled by Schirmer's outlet through Hal Leonard Music in Milwaukee, and Patelson's in New York, and are an elite, scholarly product. If you become addicted and want more, he also edited Liszt, Mendelssohn, Schubert, and Schumann, with only the Etudes, Ballades, and Preludes of Chopin available in translation.

Debussy. Durand, the classy, expensive French publisher, is patently in control here, at least for the moment until more and more Debussy moves into the public domain. Gradually, as copyright dates expire, they will all be open to competitive publication, not just the older works. Good new editions at realistic prices are beginning to creep onto the market. Each new Henle and Peters catalogue contains more of these with Edwin F. Kalmus and Dover not far behind. The Preludes are an album must, plus the individual pieces that are well known, as ones from "The Children's Corner," "Deux Arabesques," "Suite Bergamasque," and the very important "Reflets dans l'Eau", from "Images."

Handel. The Suites are enjoyable to study and sight-read and are obtainable from most publishers.

Haydn. Even those who are his detractors, for whatever reason, praise his Variations in F minor. This is printed in a handsome format by Henle. Peters sells a fine edition of the Sonatas complete in four volumes, with a fair reconciliation of the confusing Sonata numbers on the last page of Volume 1. I have only to say that these don't always agree with numbers in the Schwann record catalogue and other public print, which seems perplexing. Also these volumes are some of the most unyielding and hostile to being opened in my entire library. What is inside looks good indeed once you can gain access, but they coyly strive to remain chaste. Haydn Sonatas can be found in satisfactory selected editions available from most publishers.

Liszt. C. F. Peters is the dominant publisher here. They do an absolutely superb job in all respects. The two volumes, *Original Compositions,* are a grand place to start with Liszt, with the Etudes and Hungarian Rhapsodies following close behind. New editions are on the way from Barenwreiter and the American Liszt Society and no doubt others. We have already mentioned the Cortot editions. As with the other students' editions, they are of absolutely superior quality.

There is a certain grand-scale continuity to the album of Liszt Etudes that is comparable to the Chopin Etudes. Unlike the magisterial separateness of Sonatas as great as Beethoven's, these Liszt and Chopin works are more of a piece, the Concert Etudes, the Paganini Etudes, the Chopin Etudes. If one could sit, then start and end one of those pale green albums in a single session it would be hard to think of one other thing that could be accomplished that day which would supersede it.

Mendelssohn. A most succulent "Songs without Words" collection can be bought from the redoubtable Henle as well as any other active source. "Variations Serieux" from Schirmer is fine as is the excellent Six Preludes and Fugues, Opus 35, with the superior No. 1 available in a single edition from Schirmer.

Mozart. Ah, well. Who does *not* publish the Sonatas of Mozart? Those from Peters are excellent except that the two-volume paper-cover edition's pages defy opening. They remain in stolid defiance of the will of the player to make them lie back. I quibble — yet considering the study, practice, and performance attention these works should receive over the years — rivaling the "Well-Tempered Clavier" and Beethoven's Sonatas — it would seem that a cloth cover and solid, book-type binding would be well worth the investment, in fact a good place to start the cloth-bound commitment. In addition, here might be a good place to recommend a combined single album. I don't know how many times I have reached for one volume of a two-volume set and wanted the other. The single edition from Henle or Peters should "see one out," as the saying goes.

Also recommended is a volume of the Miscellaneous Pieces that includes some select Variations. Most publishers sell this.

Rachmaninoff. The Preludes in two books as edited by Ruth Laredo have been published at long last by Peters. The interpretive notes are helpful if slightly informal and miserly. However, the notation is all but unreadable. The staves are undersized and thus so widely spaced that the treble of one staff appears to mate with the bass above it rather than its proper bass underneath. Notes are not only minuscule but devised on an elliptical slant like hastily copied orchestra parts.

The publisher, in a most gracious and sensitive response, pleads that the cost of having new notation printed is prohibitive these days, with which I can certainly sympathize. Nonetheless, when the meager fingering is considered alongside the above, this is a most unsatisfactory edition. Not only is it not up to Peters's standards but actually looks as if the typography had retrogressed to mid-nineteenth century. I would prefer the Schirmer edition: the notation is squiggly at times as if some parts had been done in great haste, and assuredly a salutary reminder that no mechanical device nor computer is used for transcribing music onto the engraving plates. Still, it is on the whole more readable and must be our choice here.

Ravel. Much like Debussy, the gilt-edged Durand has a lock on later editions. They are nicely done, though a bit small-noted in some cases. Schirmer and some other publishers sell the earlier works that have come into public domain.

Schubert. All publishers offer the Sonatas, as might be expected. The Associate Board's three-volume set is most complete, including fragmentary works and excellent commentary by Howard Ferguson that won't have you in the aisles like Tovey and is a bit more frugal, but certainly gets the job done. I avoid the single-volume edition here, both because of the length of the Sonatas but also because of the composer's periods which simplify location of the works.

The Impromptus are widely available and should without question be secured. These are usually in a group including Opus Nos. 90 and 142, and "Moments Musicaux"; all most worthy.

Schumann. Though bargain hunters might be attracted by the inclusiveness and reasonableness of Kalmus's "Clara Schumann" edition of all of the piano solo works, they lack an attraction for this player. For one thing, they don't even look the way I think serious music should look. Agreed, they are not as bad as the Dover and other publications that try to hype the albums by enclosing them in glossy covers with fancy artwork, but they have a cheap textbook feel. Moreover, notation is ugly as well as out-of-date. There are strange gaps as well. Who would wish to devote serious study to the beguiling "Symphonic Etudes" and come screaming up to that tough finale and find that the five later variations were not included. . . *not included anywhere,* by the way.

Henle, Salabert (Cortot), and Peters have lovely Schumann editions. They offer collected works and handsome single editions, the latter being the way to go in the case of Schumann. While this composer presents a problem, as with Chopin, of wondering where to stop, your library must include Papillons, Kinderszenen, Kreisleriana, Phantasiestücke, Sonata in G minor, Humoresque, Davidsbundlertdanzen, Symphonic Etudes, and the Toccata.

Duets. For the occasion when there are two pianists on hand, the availability of some basic duet music as part of the library is a welcome resource. In order of preference would be:

Schubert	Original Compositions	Peters and Henle
Mozart	Original Compositions	Peters and Henle
Brahms	Waltzes, Hungarian Dances	Peters and Henle

Most can be obtained in cloth bindings where rapid and permanent page turning is even more important than in solo piano work.

Single Pieces. For somewhat different reasons than were advanced for stocking up on cloth-bound reference "bibles" for the library of music, some effort should be made to obtain a representation of single pieces of "performance editions," as they are sometimes called. They are easier to pull out and work on in this lighter form. They are handier and more wieldy when performing for someone. Moreover, they fill the listener with congeniality and make him more receptive when he is assured that there is no risk that you might try to plow through a whole album. Also, when the subject of traveling comes up with the hope of finding a piano somewhere, these separate pieces furnish you a mini-library of key selections to keep up your practice. For filing they can be tucked into albums of related work so that continuity in practice is not disrupted.

Due to the high cost of publishing and marketing music and the commensurate low turnover, these performance editions are becoming an endangered species. Once current stocks are used up it is likely that single editions of only the most obvious pieces will be printed and carried by dealers. Purchase while the going is good or you may never be able to pick up the single pieces you want.

Although catalogues seldom update comprehensively to show all of the single editions offered, there are still a great many published or at least still lingering on shelves of a few stores in some major cities. Even at a great distance it is a simple matter to send off a list of requested numbers to Hal Leonard, Patti, Patelson, or The Music Shop, along with your credit card information and await results.

Chapter 6

Practicing as a Way of Life

Avoid the faint of heart, the frugal of spirit, and the
meagre of intellect.

Multiplication is vexation,
Division is as bad;
The rule of three doth puzzle me,
And practice drives me mad.
Elizabethan MS (1570)

If there were but one thought I could convey with such a degree
of fervency and conviction that I could rejoice in the belief that it had
been acceptable as immutable gospel it would be that for the
amateur, practice is *not* a means to an end.

This lovely quote about amateur practice is from the French
literary critic Roland Barthes in his book, *The Grain of the Voice,*
wherein he refers to his early study of the piano with his aunt and
the atmosphere of music which surrounded him.

I haven't studied music since, I have no technique, no speed.
I did learn to read music at an early age, and my fingers follow as
best they can. So I can sight-read music, but I don't really know
how to play. Which is fine for amateur playing. Despite lagging
tempi and false notes, I still manage to attain the materiality of the
musical text, because it passes into my fingers. The sensuality of
music is not purely auditory, it is also muscular.

Thus, practice is not a means to an end. To think otherwise
would be to say that prayer was directed toward a desire or fulfillment and that the same was true of painting. Nothing could be farther from the truth. Prayer, painting, music, and other such under-

53

takings are fulfillments in and of themselves, at least for the amateur. Once the rudiments are learned, and once the elements of practice are set forth by a competent mentor, apply these words of the master speaking to his departing student in Herrigel's *Zen in the Art of Archery:*

> Even if broad seas lie between us, I shall always be with you when you practice what you have learned. I need not ask you to keep up your regular practicing, not to discontinue it on any pretext whatsoever, and to let no day go by without your performing the ceremony even without bow and arrow or at least without having breathed properly. I need not ask you because I know you can never give up the spiritual archery.... For this is what the art of archery means: a profound and far-reaching contest of the archer with himself.
>
> Perhaps you have hardly noticed it yet, ...but things will no longer harmonize as before. You will see with other eyes and measure with other measures. It has happened to me too, and it has happened to all of us who are touched by the spirit of this art.

Practice should be a joy that stands on its own two feet. Leave driven practice that aims for certain outside objectives or goals of performance to the professional and the achievers.

Louis Kentner in *Piano* writes of practicing that "You should regard [it] as a physical and mental training; it continues for your lifetime and demands the fully committed resources of body and mind."

I would take those thoughts one step further and suggest that, given some background and basic music training, practice for the amateur *is* a creative enterprise that is worth cultivating on its own for both the advancement in skills that it quite obviously instills but also for the sheer pleasure of doing it. I repeat, the sheer pleasure of doing it.

Timothy Gallwey wrote in *Inner Tennis,* "You can learn everything you need to know through awareness only of your own experience....Teachers who can help you to increase your awareness of the significant part of an experience and guide you to new experiences are performing a valuable service."

How widespread is our understanding of this contest with self, this communing with the spiritual art? This act of personal exploration is delineated by Edmund Blunden's poignant reminiscence of

World War I entitled, *Undertones of War*, wherein he describes awakening in a bivouac near Auchel in France in the most dire circumstances, "Seeing a young woman at an open window looking out in some wonder at the sudden incursion in the streets, I addressed her in the most persuasive French I could find, and she hastened down to give us food and lodging, and next day piano practice and *L'Illustration*." Next day piano practice: now there's a cultural legacy for you.

What we have been talking about here is clearly the setting aside of the act of practicing as rigor and an exercise; something odious, exclusionary, and offensively time-consuming, if not boring. I am suggesting a new definition, a new perspective on this occupation which would more appropriately be described as a calling, an enthusiasm, a commitment; more like taking religious orders but with one major difference. The disciplines are totally self-imposed and can be, at least to the lay person, just as ecstatic and blissful.

Practice, practice, practice = joy, joy, joy. But heed this warning. Practice what you feel. That is, order your practice sessions up as you would a lovely feast. Don't regard them as donnings of a hair shirt that must be suffered to obtain benefit. Relish. Enjoy. Revel.

Avoid serendipity. Establish what time you wish to work — morning, evening, or both. Order up the standard starting materials: scales, exercises (if you wish), inventions, WTC (as you will come to abbreviate Bach's Forty-eight Preludes and Fugues) baroque suites, études: they are the common springboard stuff. But even with that palette to choose from, if you don't experience a thrill of pleasure, of jubilation, and anticipation, look for a more attractive starting point for your efforts. Don't you see? It is exactly as Gallwey stated it. Choose your experience to increase your awareness. The piano is no judge of what speeds your growth as a player: certainly not this writer. *You* must delve into the treasure chest of a thousand solo piano works and lovingly pursue your practice with just those compositions that inflame your heart.

Later as your mood comes more under the control of the work you are doing you can slot in those necessary drills and chores you desire. Though the key motive is always to play well and beautifully there is no way to do this without feeling blissfully enraptured at every step of the way.

Seymour Bernstein wrote in his book, *With Your Own Two Hands*, "To my surprise, I discovered that many of [my pupils] looked upon practicing as nothing more than dutiful preparation for their lessons." Such a condition contradicts the more pleasurable, rewarding theory that the amateur should be practicing solely for his own enjoyment, enhancement, and creation of beautiful music.

Who said you must suffer? Show me where it is written that you must start off with dull, spiritless finger-twiggles. For all the dogmatic statements urging routine drilling of exercises and scales — and I know they exist — I shall produce an equal number that inspire excitement, progress, and beauty through direct study of the compositions themselves.

H. L. Mencken had a unique method of preparing for study when he was in college. He described washing his hands in warm, soapy water and drying them with a fluffy towel. He then sharpened his pencils. He scrupulously checked his pen to see that the flow of ink was adequate, finally giving his hands one last inspection front and back to see that they were worthy of the work that lay ahead. Only then did he advance toward his work table.

In front of his intended seat he would discover thirteen playing cards loosely grouped in a face down pile as if they had recently been placed there. Raising his eyes to the perimeter of the table he perceived three similar piles set forth at the remaining three quadrants of the table. Raising his eyes yet further there was revealed a fellow student seated in each of the three chairs around the table, their eyes agleam with expectant camaraderie. It is within this atmosphere of anticipation that we want to substitute our piano for Mencken's table and cardplayers.

In a recent answer to an amateur's letter, Ruth Laredo wrote in *Keyboard Classics* magazine (fall 1986), "I would suggest starting [practice] early in the day before going to work for maximum concentration. If that is at all possible, you can accomplish more if your mind is fresh." True. Let somebody else have your leftover head!

Her correspondent went on to ask about his discouragement in tackling all the "required exercises" of scales, arpeggios, Hanon, Czerny, Schmitt, etc. To which Laredo answered, "Where does it say that exercises are required? There are certain times when such warm-ups are terrific but certainly not every day, and not if you have a limited time in which to practice. It's much better to play for fun and leave exercises to the conservatory kids."

She continued in a vein so many other pianists have echoed in interviews and in writing with respect to their own development and practice procedures. "I think it is very beneficial to work on a Chopin *Etude* or *Prelude.* Such music is technically challenging and can help you more than any dry exercise can. A routine of intriguing Chopin pieces, any of the Preludes in Opus 28, for example, at a slightly slower tempo would be wonderful for the technique *as well as the soul.* And leave the Hanon in the piano bench."

If you needed more convincing, here are the words of Amherst's Dorothy Taubman from *The Piano Quarterly* (spring 1986): "I never assign exercises. I disapprove of them because they are often responsible for injuries. . . . You can't stretch the small muscles of the fingers without eventually causing damage."

I would say and shall have much more to write on that subject including a wholehearted exhortation to work on all of the Chopin Etudes and Preludes constantly as the greatest practice tools in the world above all else.

Adopting the "Student's Life"

Most adult amateurs share a common problem in thinking they have insufficient time to practice. Part of their rationale is based logically on simple arithmetic. By subtracting the hours of work, sleep, meals, toilet, shower, and usual amenities, there seems to be little time left over.

Let us remain skeptical and try to scavenge those paltry remnants of time that Bernard Berenson wrote of when he said, in *Rumor and Reflection,* that he was obsessed with the idea of standing on street corners, his cap in his hand, and begging passersby for their wasted time. If you, as an amateur, are dedicated to the idea of becoming a better pianist, it is obligatory that you grab yourself by the scruff of the neck and be ruthless with yourself and others, that you give the boot to feckless, sycophant intruders, phone callers, routine engagements, busy work, or reading of newspapers and periodicals, and let all of *them* vie for any leftover time. Let them have your brain and your willpower when they are finished with their musical commitments.

Estimable Charles Cooke is far too charitable and lenient in setting a goal of 30 minutes a day for a busy person when you consider that upwards of 120 minutes is often the length of most movie tapes (QED).

Thus the amateur would do well to remember the length of periods of study and preparation that serious students, possibly including himself, seemed to find during college days. This was in addition to substantial hours of classroom attendance, sports, and recreational and social distractions of all sorts that we all seemed to have time for. An aspiring musician practices, performs, and takes lessons incessantly if he's good and if he's committed, often six to eight hours a day and more. An athlete's life is dominated by workouts, training, and conditioning followed by competition. A writer often works creatively from four to six hours a day, then looks forward to time spent later in research, reading, assembling, and editing previous drafts. A painter paints. . . . *What on earth has happened to us as adults?* The difference in the life of students and the life of most adults rests heavily on the ceaseless swarm of alternative activities and choices that become layered upon an already complex existence. We could enumerate the curses of newspapers, radio, magazines, solitary commuting by car, television, card and video games, light sports, cheap reading, idle gossip and conversation, the monopolistic telephone itself, personal services requiring one's presence, trivial hobbies, and the pitiable addiction to shopping. These elements crowd our daily schedule with each one tugging at our sleeve and clarioning its shrill demand like so many cats yowling for their dinners.

The average college student does not have to grapple to as great an extent with so many magnates of interest as consumer buying, auto repair and maintenance transport, child care and attention, health care, lengthy social events, games, TV shows, pets, familial relations, complex investments, dominating telephone, or periodicals, to name only a few. It would be fair to say that the life of a devoted student of college level in a serious curriculum is by choice and in circumstances less fragmented by extraneous diversions.

Our culture used to embody a powerful work ethic that would render this diatribe in favor of commitment redundant. It seems that at this current stage of writing, the conventional "workplace" absorbs whatever remains of this old tradition, with none of it left over for serious pursuit of the arts by an amateur; at least one is made to feel that way.

Mostly we adults are made to feel that we are left out of the social and economic swim of things if we try to break out of this adult stereotype. To a certain extent we are. However, life is made up of choices and sacrifices, which is one of the reasons it is so rich in opportunities. However, these opportunities must be prioritized.

Your mission as a motivated amateur pianist should be to recapture insofar as possible the zeal of a dedicated student. You must find some time early in the day and later as well. You must don your surplice and take your vows. Sleep less. Most adults require only five, at the most six, hours a night. Take the advice of Arnold Bennett and (here we take cognizance of the numerous undertakings of Bennett at the height of his powers) forsake periodicals except those required in one's business, and give up newspapers altogether save for a last sleepy gander at bedtime. Order clothes by mail. Only go into a store that sells food. Exercise faster and more efficiently. Watch only meaningful programs on TV and tape those you do wish to watch and play them back at a time of your choosing (isn't that one of the reasons VCRs were invented?). Don't eat so much. Don't go anywhere or do anything unless it is important. Don't listen to anyone's advice except that of your own conscience. Never miss a day of practice even if it must be silent or consist merely of breathing correctly as the master suggested. Bear in mind what Liszt said, "If I miss a day of practice, I know it. If I miss two days, my wife knows it. If I miss five days, the public knows it."

Somewhere along the line if the amateur wants to make a success out of this piano business he has to adopt a "public be damned" attitude. It is the only way. To master any art, of which the basic six — as pointed out in Kenkō's *Essays in Idleness* — are "rites", *music,* archery, riding, calligraphy, and mathematics, it is essential to clear a lot of these insistent distractions out of the way. Certainly practicing the piano thirty minutes a day is better than nothing, but it is hardly sufficient to do more than run a few scales, whip off a baroque gigue, address some short work in progress, and gulp down a page or two of sight-reading: wholly inadequate.

To show you where we are headed, the ideal practice minimum per day would be for two hours and would include time for:

20 minutes	Bach preferred, or scales and exercises
20 minutes	Chopin Etudes or, secondarily, Preludes
20 minutes	Beethoven Sonata: alternate new and old
20 minutes	Long work in progress
20 minutes	Repertoire maintenance
20 minutes	Sight-reading

Nothing about this regimen is rigid. The segments of practice must give and take. A sure guarantee of how to do this is to swear off looking at your watch. Just guess at the time allocations; carry them in your head. Do anything you can to work within yourself: most of all, pushing aside anything to do with the external. One thing is certain, those two hours will fly by like a comet.

Some Mechanics of Practicing

Good lighting obviously means having no shadows on the music or the keyboard. Also, the atmosphere for study and concentration is sometimes more persuasive if light is directed in a circumscribed fashion onto the music and little else from a small pedestal lamp, desk lamp on the music rack, or ceiling spot. Certainly this is a matter best left to personal taste. I just happen to favor specific rather than ambient lighting, which, I might add, is a like preference in a restaurant where candles or individual table lights make me happy and, conversely, an overall drugstore glow, sad.

Music Must Be Housebroken

As partially discussed in chapter five on the basic library, do not suffer cranky, self-closing music for one brief second. Break the back of your music books as if you were busting a recalcitrant bronc. Position the book on the table with the edge of the spine down and the book held vertically. Force the covers open all the way until they touch the table, pressing and smoothing the inside of the hinge forcefully with your hand. Fold back and flatten alternating groups of three or four leaves on the left, pressing and smoothing, and then on the right, and so forth until the entire book is dividing in the middle and lies back docilely in two halves.

In severe cases I have even sacrilegiously placed the book on the floor and stood on it. Justification resides in the fact that having an inanimate object interrupt play and concentration is worse than the plague and deserves extreme countermeasures. This phenomenon poses a convincing argument for most sewn bindings. In the case of some frequently used albums, like Chopin's Etudes and Preludes, this page-turning problem makes a convincing argument for buying the cloth-bound books previously referred to. The most difficult and exasperating music to handle is the cheap albums with a single stitching of all pages right down the middle. Buying music in such a form is like throwing money away. There is no way to make it lie flat on the music rack—ever.

Beautiful Tone, the First Commandment

What are we working toward? One of the objectives beyond our own enjoyment is surely to give others pleasure, even if they are unseen and can only hear the piano music from outside the room in which it is being played, or only if we imagine there are those who can hear it. From the auditor's point of view there is little that will stir the romantic imagination more than becoming aware that attractive piano music is heard through an open pair of French doors. The very idea that someone is sitting alone indoors and generating beautiful sounds is a great promoter of powerful inner feelings.

Abby Whiteside's *Mastering the Chopin Etudes* is admired because of her success as a teacher. Her notes and comments are the result of fifty years of inspiring progress in students. She regards the Chopin Etudes as the seminal practice work. The editors state in the foreword, "She never changed, nor had any reason to change, her opinion that anyone who could play all of these Etudes well would be equipped to handle any technical demands that he might encounter. Therefore, every student was encouraged to study one Etude after another."

The stressing of reading music in the early stages was a mistake according to Whiteside, who felt that there should be more taught by rote and more emphasis on transposition so "that the ear was always in command of the playing . . . [the music student] should be an aural learner rather than a visual learner."

Hear what Robert Dunn, former Dean of the Boston Conservatory, had to say on this same point in an article in *Piano Classics* magazine (1987). "Your ears must work with your fingers—quick ears, with fingers less-than-quick—to supply impression to your brain. You must become ear-alert and touch-alert to what your practice is recording (in your head)."

Sylvia Craft, well-known music executive, writes that her first teacher, Emil Friedberger, would say, "Always think about the desired sound *before* striking the keys."

So bear in mind this extra-dimensional vision of your playing. Of course, stop to mark the music, repeat difficult passages when they occur — but still maintain some sense of artistry in your performance. As you play some Preludes and Fugues of Bach, or the Etudes and Preludes of Chopin, always perform them as if you had a listener. Consider them as miniature programs for friendly outsiders. Project your image of the music in a theatrical manner, not as if it were some dull, flat exercise like tugging on the oars of a rowing machine.

The Metronome

This is a device that is the subject of some controversy, with some teachers and methods advocating it, and some not. This ambivalence might be likened to the scales versus exercises argument or the études versus preludes argument. No doubt there are students and situations that call strongly for metronomes when we consider the difficulty of always maintaining steady rhythm.

The problem is easily resolved. Have a metronome available. At a specific stage in the learning of certain kinds of compositions, there is no question that a metronome can be a useful tool to speed the learning process and measure one's progress. Take, for example, Chopin's Prelude, Opus 28, No. 16, in B-flat minor, a virtuoso piece and perhaps the difficult prelude, and likely outside the scope of the average amateur. It can only be approached through painstakingly slow drill at gradually increased speeds. There are devices for gaining access to this kind of material of which we will speak later, but No. 16 is a good specimen for the potential use of the metronome, almost calling to mind Sam Saxe's snail's pace jazz drills. The notes and phrases are not that unfathomable, but holding them together with a convincing rhythm is. That is where the metronome comes in.

The standard method is, of course, to begin each project at a comfortable, playable speed, no matter how slow (half speed possibly); mark it; increase it three or four times; and try again another day. Rachmaninoff is said to have practiced Chopin's famous knuckle-busting "Etude in Thirds," Opus 26, No. 6, in G-sharp minor, over and over at a lugubriously slow tempo for routine practice. This was at a time when he was considered one of the greatest pianists in the world.

At the Tchaikovsky International Piano Competition of 1986, one semifinalist began that Etude most impressively with the initial trill of thirds and lapsed into an insane time warp or muscle or brain warp where he couldn't unlock the rest of the piece and merely sat there trilling away for what seemed like an hour. The ting of a little bell eventually broke his trance and he was led from the stage in abysmal humiliation. I would hate to think of that as "metronome block."

In addition to tough pieces there are those where the tempo tends to wander. This could be the case in practicing the slow movement of, say, Beethoven's Sonata in A Major, Opus 2, No. 2. We are looking for a "Big Ben" conducted feel to this segment and submitting to a metronome might assist in obtaining the effect of a string quartet, thereby executing measured pizzicatos with punctilious accuracy.

Yet another valuable application, also in slow work, is in wending one's perilous way through the obfuscating notation of, say, the opening of Liszt's "Funerailles." Here the use of thirty-second-note clusters and differing rests can give trouble and occasionally boggle the ear. Some nice penciled beat marks above beats one, two, three, and four, plus the metronome beat setting a defined, steady tempo could help us see the light.

Interpretation

The student must often decide between two clearly defined modes of interpretation. We can often see an example of this when reading what two stellar writers about the piano have to say regarding the famous octave passages in Chopin's Polonaise in A-flat, Opus 53.

Donald N. Ferguson in *Piano Music of Six Great Composers* writes, "Taken at the intended tempo (maestoso), Chopin was distressed even in his day, by the speed bugs. The piece is less difficult than it sounds. Though it is possible and profitable to play it in a forbiddingly dynamic manner, it is legitimately within the right of every student of reasonable advancement to try his hand at it. . . . Properly the tempo does not change at the E [M]ajor section."

Louis Kentner in *Piano* writes, "[The polonaises] should be played in a heroic, aggressive, even swaggering style. A healthy exhibitionism in, for example, the famous octave passage of the Grande Polonaise in A flat is not at all misplaced, for this piece should not be made to sound like a dull octave study (however efficiently played) but rather a tremendous crescendo with a crashing climax at the end."

The amateur is probably better off following Ferguson in this.

Earl Wild, the virtuoso pianist, speaks in the March/April 1986 issue of *Keyboard Classics,* of the problems of addressing romantic music. "I always ask my students what the music means. . . . Think about it and give me an idea or an image. For example, when playing the Dante Sonata by Liszt, one might imagine the illustrations of Doré, with all their overplayed drama and heroics . . . or [a student's] own emotional life while playing the Petrarch Sonata. It helps to have something in mind when you play . . . something to cling to."

Can we resolve these seeming conflicts? Scrupulous play in first readings versus grasp of musical concept? Conservatism of interpretation versus bold swagger? Of course. We are going to find the best for us. We are going to do all these things and yet see them recede just as the Zen master has the student, "learn to wait properly. . . . By letting go of yourself, leaving yourself and everything yours behind you so decisively that nothing more is left of you but a purposeless tension."

We will read slowly but not without an aural image, and we will work up a difficult piece like the A-flat Polonaise in a manageable tempo but with a bit of dash.

In Herrigel's *Zen in the Art of Archery,* the Zen master silently conducted his pupil into a dimly lit practice hall. He had his student place a thin taper in the sand below the target which remained unilluminated. It was too dark to see the outlines. The master had only the taper to point the way to the target. At first he "danced" the ceremony of preparation, suggesting some mental imagery and key bodily preparation. Next he let loose his first arrow out of dazzling brightness into deep night. The pupil could tell from the sound that it had hit the target.

An almost comparable situation exists when serving the ball in tennis. An average player has very little trouble in propelling a ball to the opponent's side that both clears the net and lands within the service area. If the ball's trajectory were to be drawn out as a side view showing court surface, net, and base and service lines all to scale, it would show that the ball had to travel in a flattened arc of about eighty feet and land in an eight-inch-wide safe slot. Any above-average player could probably serve a high percentage of serves into the correct area *even if he were blindfolded.*

Looked at in this way, it is not a major miracle that an ordinary mortal can seat himself in front of a piano keyboard and by a curious reliance on ear, sight, muscle-memory, nervous system, and bravado almost intuitively conspire to produce complex musical sounds that are pleasing to the human ear. This art is close to sorcery and certainly much more complicated than the serve in tennis. Its practice is deserving of cultivation and reverence.

Whatever your musical aspirations might be, whatever your repertoire selections might be, apply yourself first and foremost to the act of making beautiful music. Do this by first comprehending what the music intends to say, what it is about. Think exclusively of yourself as the interpreter of that utterance. Next, fully engage your conscious mind in order to bring this about by anticipating the sounds you wish to create. Imagine them.

Later your musical speech will become like a foreign language learned as a child in which you are proficient enough to both speak and think without having to translate in your head. Key signatures, phrase markings, fingerings, even the very notation will become like so many secondary road markers on a familiar highway. You will be operating in a Zen mode like that fantastic arrow let loose in the dark. Your automatic pilot will take over. You will be letting loose of yourself. For the moment, though, we are considering the act of good practicing and not yet that rarefied plane of intuitive, inspired, almost automatic playing. Engage your conscious mind. Think. Feel.

Body Movement and Rotation

Technically, Whiteside and Matthay excel in these areas and should be read and studied repeatedly, for you will want to know how to alter tone to achieve the aural objective you have initiated. Once you realize the direct influence the torso, upper and lower arms, and breathing have over tone production, you will be following the watchful guidance of Whiteside who writes, "you know you *have* a torso, set it free and exult in its freedom."

Picture Ivan Lendl standing like a post and swinging at a tennis ball as if he were sweeping a beer can from a table. Hard to visualize, isn't it? What we see him do is take a position, retract his legs like springs, then rotate and lift his torso and legs and simply allow his arms—like the master's bow and the pianist's fingers—to push the ball at whatever angles, at whatever speed, and with whatever gyrations he wishes. As Whiteside says, "Let the big levers do the work."

Rhythm

What does the ear start with? At the most primitive level it would be hand claps, drum beats, thumping of some kind — rhythm. Wynton Marsalis presented a master class in the trumpet on the Public Broadcasting System with a full complement of musicians plus an active class of students, all more or less "in the round." He started the rhythm section going with drums, bass, guitar, and piano, then suggested some riffs from the wind instruments and in no time at all had organized them all into a full-blown jazz ensemble.

The seriousness with which a firm rhythm needs to be taken was pointed out by Leschetizky, whose student, Gotfried, reported in an early diary, "His chief criticism was only that I am not firm enough in my rhythm. I say, 'only.' It is to laugh. He assured me this not keeping time will trouble me all my life, but that I might circumvent that weakness by intellectual means. That lesson may be important for my whole life" (*The Piano Quarterly*, winter 1987/88, page 45).

Abby Whiteside suggests, "Play a waltz with the emotional response primarily attached to the melodic line, and there will be no waltz which will captivate the audience. A waltz is a dance first of all. Play the fundamental basses with the lilt and grace one sees and feels when watching a great dancer or skater, and the melody will be more beautiful and graceful, and the delight of the audience will be instant in its response."

It is the same thing, you see. Production of the music all starts with rhythm. These are the building blocks of your performance:
1. rhythm;
2. bodily involvement (torso, arms, breathing);
3. tonal concept (heavy ear anticipation).

Left Hand and Bass

Alicia de Larrocha states in *Piano Classics* (1988), "The left hand is more important than the right. It's the most important hand in everything, in balance of sound, in rubato, in style. The left hand is like a column that holds the whole building, the whole monument. The melody is nothing, really — just the first thing the ear captures."

Now we have music. Oh, yes, the melody can be added as an embellishment, yet it is what most people think is most important since it is what they hear first and remember most.

Reference can be made to the glamorous mainsail of a racing sailboat. The working sails forward of the mast are just that, the various Genoa jibs, working jibs, spinnakers, and drifters, which provide 80 percent of the forward drive of the boat. The mainsail provides balance and a nice broad expanse of cloth on which to display the racing numbers. It is mostly for show—like the melody. The real driving force is elsewhere.

Thus we add a fourth building block, the left hand and bass. We now have our structure.

Another analogy could be in constructing a house. Though entirely visual, we might start with the architectural plans (composition), then the components of the concrete foundation (bass), the airy roof and overhanging eaves (melody) and, finally, some well-proportioned doors and windows (rhythm). The trim, cabinets, tile, flooring, wallpaper, and paint constitute the decorative elements (inner voice and ornaments).

There are certain procedural and physical controls you can institute to make your practicing more meaningful. Relaxation has a high priority. However, if you feel yourself becoming tense, how can you release the pressure? Much as in tennis or any other sport or endeavor, you can take a little off your serve, so to speak. You can ease up and reduce speed so you don't make the same amount of errors and allow your body and mind to set a congenial pace.

This control problem is thoroughly addressed in a deceptively short article in *The Piano Quarterly* issue of Summer 1989, by George Kochevitsky and Edward McCallson. They write of the alternating of excitation and inhibition, pointing out that pianists cannot play faster than they can think! They suggest practicing difficult passages in short units and stopping intentionally to grasp the image of the next unit. Eventually units are combined, then eliminated. Why not try this system on either a cadenza in a Chopin Nocturne (D-flat, for example) or any of the Scherzi including the one in Sonata No. 3? You should discover the validity of this scheme at once.

In case you are hung up on the matter of technique and whether or not you have sufficiently steeped yourself in this mystical element of preparation, you might welcome a soothing philosophy from the same concise article. The authors quote a remark of Ferruccio Busoni who said that pianists who have acquired an elementary vocabulary (have) "a bundle of pick locks and skeleton keys." Our authors go on to say, and "Having developed these half-ready products . . . will necessitate some modification of the technical approach." So much for giving undue obeisance to the icon of technique.

The path of learning these writers advocate starts with the development of the mind as a control point for the central nervous system. By means of the nerve paths, this exerts its influence on the finer sensitivities of the finger movement, leaving the large finger muscles about as important as they are to a diamond cutter or a brain surgeon.

Other tips are to change the order in which you practice different pieces or blocks of pieces. Variety of sequence will persuade you to look at your material through fresh eyes.

Generally finish pieces that you start, partly as a character builder, and partly as assurance that you've taken the whole composition into your consciousness. These disciplines are helpful to the whole goal-achievement role of practice.

Chapter 7

Practicing: Some Fundamentals

New Material

The tension that is sometimes apparent when embarking on the study of new material can often be relieved by following some basic structural clues in the notation and phrasing and using these breaks as physical and mental signals to breathe.

A tennis player will often find himself out of breath at the end of a hotly contested point because, odd as it may seem, he has neglected breathing during the exchange of shots and has unconsciously held his breath. This increases the tension of the situation and magnifies the potential for error. In *Zen in the Art of Archery*, similarly stated, "The breathing in, like the breathing out, is practiced again and again by itself with the utmost care. One does not have to wait long for results. The more one concentrates on breathing, the more the external stimuli fade into the background." To do otherwise not only causes strain, shoulder heaving to catch the breath, undue pressure on the player, but most important of all, a failure to relax, which is the prime requisite of all. The parallel between these examples and fruitful keyboard performance is obvious.

Recall, if you will, the Ingmar Bergman film *Autumn Sonata*. Ingrid Bergman plays a successful concert pianist who joins her untalented daughter, Liv Ullman, at the piano. They share a playing of Chopin's Prelude, Opus 28, No. 2, in A minor. Ullman displays her tenseness by weaving her stiff shoulders around like a cobra preparing to strike and perfectly conveys the barriers caused by failing to let herself go, breathe, and relax. Bergman, of course, simulates the consummate artist as she sits poised and calm and seems to let the piece play itself like the good Zen master's arrow finding the target in the shadows.

Always remember that a composition is made up of rhythm, bass, melody, and harmony. Prove this by establishing a steady rhythm, then playing only the top and bottom notes of a simple waltz and experience your ear filling in the harmonies as if they were being played.

It is worth emphasizing this contribution of the ear. Abby Whiteside spoke of it when she wrote, "Observe the ease and accuracy of pupils who have learned to play by ear. Their skill is never attained by those who learned dependent on the eye. . . . The pupil who has learned music by the way it sounds *hears the tone when he looks at the symbol.* The movements that make this imagined tone audible are directed by the ear" (*Mastering the Chopin Etudes,* p. 157).

As a general rule, do not choose a tempo at which you cannot execute the entire piece. Naturally there are exceptions. One can imagine a piece embodying a short single passage, such as a cadenza, that always causes stumbling no matter how many times it is practiced.

Take the advice of Casadesus to his pupils, "Do not try to play faster than you can play notes accurately. To do otherwise is to ingrain the bad habit of the mistaken notes." Such a procedure violates the rule of keeping a steady tempo throughout, but in such a case it is absurd to play an entire section at a snail's pace all for a measure or two of great difficulty. Be reasonable. Most rules are made to be broken some time; they are merely guide posts after all. A good example of this potential violation of maintaining a steady tempo would be Chopin's Prelude, Opus 28, No. 24, when it comes to the descending chromatic triplet thirds near the end.

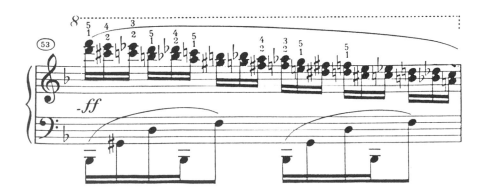

A solution in the prelude is to effect a slight ritardando in the measure before the thirds. Slightly accent the last three octaves. Then start the descent rather slowly, to find your seat in the saddle, so to speak. Be meticulous about the 5/1 "unlocking" fingering. Then gather speed as you go along until you have increased to the original tempo.

Another killer passage is the tricky 52–55 bars of the Polonaise Fantasie. It is virtually impossible for the amateur to keep this passage up to a tempo consistent with the rest.

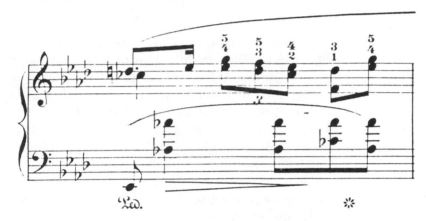

Of course the key is mastering the tricky 5/4, 5/3 fingering, but this is easier said than done, even at slow speeds. Employing the "agogic" or leaning effect may get you through the worst of it. Similarly, keep fingering rigidly consistent, and emphasize the short four- and five-note phrases as marked to gain control of this part of the work.

Regard also Beethoven's Sonata, Opus 2, No. 3. Tovey issues a warning right off the bat on that one. We have descending thirds arranged in two-measure couplets with sizable skips and chromatic modulations downward — a lot to think about. Just slow things down before proceeding, take a nice breath, and let it happen at a comfortable tempo. Try to establish the original tempo before you complete the passage.

When addressing *new material,* read it over silently first, even away from the keyboard — in bed, if you choose. In fact, if you are deprived of a piano for any length of time, take comfort in the fact that some progress can be derived from silent reading of piano music. This implies more than just staring at the notes and following the melody. It means fully conceptualizing an approximation of the key (quite possible for even those who do not have perfect pitch), rhythmic structure, harmonic patterns, tempo, potential pitfalls, even certain fingerings and "hand-sets," so that you come to know the piece before you've pressed down a single note.

We must have this "musical concept" in mind before anything. There come to mind several examples of gratuitous assumption of ignorance that justice deserves to have put to rest. First, I recall Arthur Rubinstein, in a film biography shown on PBS, castigating pianists of his time in general for not "understanding" or correctly "interpreting" Chopin's Etude, Opus 25, No. 11 (called by some "Wind Study," or "Winter Wind," or some such spurious nickname) as he did. Whereupon he demonstrated that the bass melodic line was to be emphasized over the chromatic breezes up above. Now I ask you, where would one find those who think otherwise? Similarly a great point was made in the Australian film *My Secret Ambition*, of a talented outback wunderkind who outclassed her gorgeous school chum because she knew how to "interpret" Schubert's Impromptu Opus 90, No. 3, in G-flat. The film conveyed that she could find the melody, while her beautiful cohort was too busy trying to remember the notes to waste time on prolonging the held tones of the theme. All this confusion would be akin to giving equal value to all right-hand notes of Chopin's popular A-flat Waltz and looking hurt if some wiseacre recommended stressing every third eighth note. Such quantum disregard of, or obliviousness to, the realities of what one sees indicated on the printed page can only signal a fatuousness or naïveté on the part of the practitioner; neither of which need be considered seriously here.

Just prior to playing the work for the first time, note the words of Frank Merrick from his *Practicing the Piano:*

> The first physical observance is always to touch the keys before pressing them down, because hitting them from a distance (even a slight one) reduces precision with regard to the sound coming at the right moment, with the right volume (not only total volume, but also that of the melody note and balance with those that harmonize with it), and without a smudge. The second physical observation is that habit of instantaneous relaxation of any superfluous pressure that may have been momentarily necessary for the "ff" chords.

Then start playing slowly, being sure to maintain a very steady tempo. Strive for note accuracy. Consider what Robert Dunn says in his article in *Piano Classics* (spring 1988),

> Your brain acts as a computer, registering sensations from your ears. Together, your ears and brain retain every impression they receive, especially *first* impressions; their novelty makes them indelible.... [I]n other words, you'd rather get it right the *first* time.
>
> It is at the moments *between* tones that the brain *records* both the touch and sound, and this is when the real work of practice takes place. The brain needs each "spacer" moment to learn. This is why we must never be too fast in the early stages of learning a piece, and why we should slightly exaggerate our counting of the beats between the notes we play and hold.

Demand this note accuracy of yourself. Feel everything. Keep your eyes searching all around for those vital dynamic markings, phrase marks, crescendi, ritardandi, etc. Ask yourself if the tone you are producing is really attractive and what you had intended, not just a copy of the written music. Does it sound like what you wish to express? Does your thumb attempt to bring out some legato inner voicing that might easily be mistaken for a cello? Does your treble sing as it should? Does your bass line sound sonorous and bowed? Is your rhythm convincing? Is your foot careless on the pedal, causing blurred notes and overlapping harmonies? Is the effect beautiful?

This is an ideal time to remind ourselves of those provocative words of Tobias Matthay, "The piano does not need the practice. It is we who need the practice." That is a Zen thought if I ever heard one.

While almost anyone writing on this subject recommends *slow practice*, we would benefit from Abby Whiteside's cautionary thought about this when she writes, "Accuracy, of course, cannot be ignored, but it can better be achieved after the musical conception has jelled. . . . Let beauty work its charm first. . . . The demand for accuracy in hitting the keys forces attention on single tones and does not allow the attention to skim through for the important ideas and, thus, develop the physical habits that are right for projecting the musical idea as a whole."

Sight-Reading

Let us examine sight-reading material that because of our un-familiarity might cause us to sink into a quagmire of uncertain tempi and discouraging mistakes. Consider that slow sight-reading and slow regular practice do not have to sound non-musical. Claude Frank in an interview with Adele Marcus in her book, *Great Pianists Speak*, says, "There is absolutely no substitute for slow practice.... This slow practice should be very musical. Thre are very few instances in which slow mechanical practice is beneficial. Musical slow practice is the key."

In his book, *With Your Own Two Hands,* Seymour Bernstein writes, "I am convinced that the correction of this deficiency ... must take top priority in musical education, not only because sight-reading enables one to grasp a piece as a whole but, more important, because it trains the memory and sharpens the powers of concentration."

It is possible to perform a piece at any rate of speed short of the slowest crawl. If a steady rhythm is adhered to and an attractive musical image is conceived, it should make for a convincing if not exhilarating performance. Take a very simple piece like this Scarlatti Sonata marked "Andante."

Horowitz often began a major concert with just this sort of selection. Rendered with a tentative, varying beat, this would fail all criteria for riveting devoted listener interest. In his hands, however, and taken at a determined funeral stalk, if you like, it could reveal its dramatic lines fully and leave the audience enthralled. The same could be said for his typical encore, "Traumerai." So glance forward in the work you undertake, select a tempo that can *nearly* survive the most difficult passage, clap it into irons, and become Horowitz at the keyboard rather than the amateur you are. Pretend there is someone standing outside your window and impress him with the artistry of your piece. While practicing always *feel* and *play* as if you are performing for others, *particularly* when playing slowly.

Earlier we spoke of silent study of new material, including evaluation of the harmony. It may not be necessary to decode the whole work in this silent reading, since many of the patterns may be familiar or repeated. However, a fundamental understanding of the knottier chordal and passage sequences cannot help but speed up the reading and comprehension when the keyboard is reached.

An example of an "open sesame" situation would be Chopin's Prelude, Opus 28, No. 8, in F-sharp minor, where we encounter a two-measure phrase with two dotted half-note chords of the tonic followed by one of the dominant, then back to the tonic again.

Molto agitato

This accompaniment is a murmuring design of very light notes in a repetitive "hand-set" with an appoggiatura-like configuration. This crude visual analysis can precede actual playing and provide a solid clue of what is going on. If that patter continues, which it more or less does for all except a short eight-bar release, this brief study of a tiny segment should unlock the structure of the whole composition. If you really want the clue as to what it should sound like, listen to the Martha Argerich recording and her handling of the right-thumb melody line.

There is no reason why this technique cannot be applied to any selection, and it should be. One can tolerate an occasional element of surprise when one is farther into a work, but the point here is to foresee the shock and trauma of the unexpected and allow the performer to commence with maximum confidence and be able to let go of himself. As the Zen master admonished his student, "You do not wait for fulfillment, but brace yourself for failure. So long as that is so, you have no choice but to call forth something *yourself* that ought to happen *independently* of you."

I like William S. Newman's ambitious advice about sight-reading when he writes, "Read whole volumes through. Naturally there might be inaccessible parts, but absorb the body of the work. Jot down notes of your reactions." Those whole volumes might easily be the Bach *Well-Tempered Clavier*, Mozart and Beethoven Sonatas, Chopin Mazurkas, Brahms *Miscellaneous Piano Pieces*, and Debussy Preludes for the extra hardy.

Marking Music

Treat music like paperback books and research materials. Get tough. Anytime you hear a piece of piano music or read about it in a book or newspaper review, write something about it on your copy. Especially if someone plays a piece for you, make notes about the performance. I use the right-hand corner of the first page for these comments about performances. After a while these scribblings become marvelous sagas of my experiences with that piece. As the actual notation becomes part of your subconscious the notes and markings remain. Here are my notes from the top of Schumann's Phantasiestücke:

"Hambro (Leonid — on his former radio show) played three recordings: (1) Susan Starr — affected, pauses; (2) Murray Perahia — simple, baroque style, good continuity; (3) Martha Argerich — faster, but slowed down later on, best, simplest . . . . A ribbon of sound. . . . Very deliberate . . . airy . . . long lines."

In the left-hand corner over the key signature and tempo indication I inscribe my own notes for playing. Not curiously many of these same comments and warnings appear on more than half the music I own:

"Not too fast . . . Steady rhythm . . . Singing Tone . . ." Bottom up."

Tempo Markings. My sign for the suggested tempo if, say, "T–#60." This warns me that there is no sense in starting the piece much faster than I can play measure number 60. Donald Tovey in his notes usually singles out these "control" points and is particularly good on that score. However, that is one of the things to determine for yourself, since one man's easy knock-off of a run in thirds is another man's octave glissando.

Metronome Settings. I mark these pretty obviously with most often a quarter-note indication like 70–80, giving myself a high and low setting.

Breathing. Simple as it seems, this mark, "B," reminds me to take breath. It can mean one of two things. First, it is cautionary for a piece that requires a particularly superhuman effort to free yourself and let go. Second, it can be inserted between phrases where I feel it is important to have a slight separation, sort of the opposite of an agogic "leaning." It signals a spot where I want to make certain not to create an impression of a merger between two phrases that might prevent the musical thought from getting across distinctly.

Emphasis. Circles appear around dynamic markings all over the place, particularly when there is a dramatic change. Anytime there is a "subito" I might miss or not emphasize sufficiently, I circle or underline it. The same goes for sforzandos. Also arrows and yellow highlight marking pens find frequent use in illuminating inner voices. This can occur in baroque fugues and in all music where we need reminders of these marvelous interior voices. Nothing in longer notation or critical markings suggests the importance of the marvelous inner voice, as in Chopin's Waltz in C# minor (Op. 64, No. 2).

Hand Transfers and Crossovers. These are another natural for
"R.H." or "L.H." markings. To avoid a tangle, reminders of which
hand goes over the other are nowhere more needed than in Brahms's
Opus 76, No. 1.

Difficult Passages. The two marks shown below are used to
enclose particularly troublesome sections of a work. Charles Cooke
suggests this device in his previously recommended *Playing the
Piano for Pleasure.* I use them frequently for delineating small sections that need lots of extra work. When time is limited I can identify
them quickly. An extra fillip is to assemble a list of the page numbers
on which these occur—if there are not too many, that is—setting
them forth on the first page. In cases of limited time or intensified
practice, you can go right to these worst-case areas and woodshed
them, as in Liszt's Sonata in B minor:

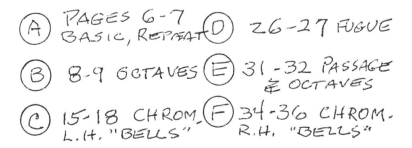

Enharmonic Markings. This and the next item are as close to
cheating as I will admit to getting. That is to mark a chord with its

enharmonic equivalent. Take, for example, a C-flat or D-sharp chord with so many accidentals camouflaging it that you feel you are apt to be derailed—forced to stop and figure it all out. I tend to label such snakepits with their simpler enharmonic equivalents. Thus, C-flat becomes (B) and D-sharp becomes (E-flat). Then I don't have to waste time deciphering things. Such a substitution for the real thing should be surrounded by parenthesis just to show that you know better in case someone calls you on it as in this Scriabin Etude.

Notes Off the Staff. I also cheat in identifying notes that are so far above or far below the staff that identifying them might cause a delay in playing the piece. I merely write down the name of the note. Simple. I just feel that it is a kind of notational conceit on the part of the composer anyway not to show 8va or 16va over a note nearer the staff, so I retaliate by greeting one impertinence with another.

False Trills. These are a merging of sounds to create the effect of a seemingly continuous trill combined with an intermittent melody executed by the same hand. This is not unlike a juggler who fakes the standard three-ball movement by lightly tossing up one ball in each hand and every so often tossing one of them higher. Here is the effect written out in Liszt's Hungarian Rhapsody No. 12:

Ornaments. Ornaments need to be amplified most of the time, at least where the editor has not thoughtfully written them out in footnotes. They can be an imperfect science at best, even though much is written in books about their execution. It is best to rehearse any recurring figures and write down some clue as to how you are going to play them, so the next time through your memory will be jogged as to whether you start on the same note or the one above. An expanded, ballooned drawing off to the side like a bubble of cartoon dialogue will do the job, or you can just spell out the notes.

Scales in Passage Work. If some passage work suggests a scale as in the following example from Chopin's Waltz in A-flat, even if there are extraneous notes added or subtracted, I just show the main scale for orientation.

Diminished Chords. Because of the frequency with which diminished chords are used in effecting modulation and in other instances to create harmonic richness and transitions, I often identify these chords. This is especially useful when they move up or down chromatically, since accidentals can pop up all over the place and confuse the issue which is otherwise quite simple. The shortcut I use is a small arrow up or down with "Cr" to show a chromatic change, here shown with Chopin's Etude, Opus 10, No. 3 in E:

Fingering. I tend to select editions that include printed fingering by the editors. I fully recognize that some crimes have been committed in this area.

Editors have come in for a good deal of criticism on account of bad, unrealistic fingering. My experience with printed fingerings has generally been acceptable. I simply keep a pencil handy to jot in changes when they are called for.

Fingering in most editions is only indicated once, which is the first time the passage occurs. Since the most elephantine of memories is apt to forget these markings when the same phrases recur several pages down the road, it is best to mark any significant identical fingerings every time they are printed in the work with a few finger numbers.

A group of pieces that pose as prime examples of a need for this requirement would be the Chopin Scherzos where a fumble in the fingering (naming measure No. 338 of the second Scherzo in B-flat minor as one paltry example) can precipitate a pratfall into the orchestra pit. Cortot's Salabert editions are an exception to this miserly fingering practice, wherein all repeated passages are duly accompanied by the repeated fingerings. Vive la France!

Fingering is underrated as a catalyst in facile sight-reading since it is thought to be something to be worked on after one begins the formal study of a piece. The point is not that it will speed along the initial readings, nor that it is needed to make the treatment credible, but merely that you can train yourself to be more aware of finger markings right along with the notes, rests, phrasing, dynamics, and other indications if you accustom yourself to reading them. After all, they are part of the whole notational message, even if they are most often added by an editor.

Fingering can be valuable when it is not overdone, as in long scale-like passages such as Schubert's Impromptu Opus 90, No. 2. Precious few clues to fingering are needed here, whereas in Chopin's Etudes most of us need plenty of them.

Schnabel's sometimes quirky fingerings in his edition of the Beethoven Sonatas have become legendary, yet they are interesting. He doesn't claim to have used them consistently. Great pianists alter fingering all the time to change the sound they wish to produce. The rest of us are well advised to work out a safe approach and *stick with it*. Mark the music!

Setting aside scale-like ascending or descending hand-sets (as in Beethoven's Sonata Opus 2, No. 3, in the final movement), there are numerous occasions (as in Beethoven's Sonata Opus 7, in E-flat, the final movement trio) where seemingly unorthodox fingering is adopted because of being able to maintain consistent hand-to-keyboard relationship every time the figure recurs. The same is true in the Appassionata final movement as this example (taken from Tovey's edition) shows:

Heavens! someone will react. It seems possible to place the third finger under the fourth even if the fourth is elevated on a black key. Someone is wrong. The fingering originated with von Bülow, and the pedigree is intact all the way down to our day. You have only to look toward Beethoven's later sforzando development of this accented second beat to comprehend the efficacy of this fingering. After you overcome an initial discomfort and have worked with this fingering a few times, you will wonder how you would have done it any other way. If we fly a flag of respect for this seemingly awkward frog-hop we will be rewarded by a remarkably durable hand-set that allows for both facile playing and a nice fresh attack when it is called for. This device enables us to retain a virtual manual "casting" of our original sequence. Once locked in, it permits an infinite number of repeats without strain — and quite rapid ones, too — as long as we do not alter the fingering.

Notes on Technique

There are some basic truths like sitting in a comfortable, relaxed position. However, I like what Garrick Ohlsson says in David Dubal's *Reflections from the Keyboard* (p. 250), when he lets fly at mannerisms: "You see kids who look like they still play with a coin on the back of their hand, or ones who look like they're swimming when they play." I can recall seeing that deplorable, sappy windmilling of the arms, wrists, and floppy hands, and how unpolished and imbecilic it makes the performer look. As an exception to prove the rule, I can point to the exciting jazz pianist Bobby ("Wild Man") Enriquez, who has developed a style that he exhibits while standing that combines both swimming *and* dancing. It works magnificently for him but presents a good argument for remaining docile during your serious classical performances.

There are numerous selections that require executing scales in thirds and sixths. To name only a few examples, there is Chopin's Nocturne in G Major, Opus 38, No. 2; Prelude Opus 28, No. 24; Berceuse; Andante Spianato; Liszt's Concert Etude No. 2; Liszt's Paganini Variations, Opus 6, 4th Variation; Brahms's Paganini Variations, Book 2, No. 1, and numerous others.

Chopin's Etude in G-sharp minor, Opus 25, No. 6, is the magnum opus, although there are many others. These thirds are infinitely harder than routine scales and should be undertaken at the earliest stages of your commitment. Any delay in their study will really inhibit later development, even the playing of such an otherwise simple piece as Chopin's Impromptu No. 3 in G-flat. The sixths are just a shade less tricky because of the more extended finger position, but both warrant heavy work.

Frank Merrick urges us on our way to mastery of thirds and sixths with this goading statement: "The aspiring student should hasten on to double thirds long before his single notes reach a high standard, for they are muscularly strengthening, they give the mind more occupation per semiquaver then the single notes, and their execution automatically keeps all five fingers closer to the keys (a desirable thing in playing every kind of passage)."

The reason the little fifth finger of the right hand is used sparingly in sight-reading is that it offers no easy escape for continuation beyond it by means of a convenient thumb-pass. It often presents a point of no return without a vertical hop of the whole hand when you may least desire it. Once you come to rest, you're stopped. But this stepchild of sight-reading can become the blessed scion of consecutive thirds and sixths where it can unblock these series of notes by its frequent use. In fact a useful mark in these precarious sequences is 5/1 or 5/2 perhaps circling them for emphasis.

Voicing. This is the most subtle of effects whereby the pianist must "bow" all parts of a movement. That is, he must think in an absolutely linear mode. Of course, this is done in baroque music, but usually with the benefit of fairly rapid movement of the parts and little pedaling. Romantic voicing is a simulation of the slow movement of a string quartet and requires the utmost finesse. No better example can be given than the Lento from Chopin's "Fantasia":

Inner Voices

Discovering inner lines can be one of the most fascinating parts of our learning process. The composer may not want these subtle lines signaled too clearly and may prefer to leave their emphasis to the pianist's interpretive skills. Thus these voices are often marked "sotto voce," to alert the pianist to their existence and the fact that the composer has cooked up something special besides the single melody line. More often than not he has left the degree of the inner voice exposure up to the artistry of the pianist. The extra voices comprise an element of interior richness that weaves like a thread of precious gold through the more dominant fabric of the composition.

The training ground for making these finds is obviously the polyphonic music of Bach. Next, your own ear and reading sensibilities can help in cultivating an awareness of the lovely interlacing melodies. Naturally the imaginative and talented professional is adept at unearthing and exploiting these interior nuances that normally lie buried within a piece. The composer, editors, and players all take a good whack at these tones, frequently notating them capriciously as seems to be the case with Chopin and Chopin editions, where some copies of the Prelude, Opus 28, Number 19 in E-flat show the significant melody line with stems of quarter notes and others do not. Is the slow movement of the 3rd Sonata to be played verbatim with the longer notes physically held down according to the indicated notation? How about Etude, Opus 10, No. 3 in E Major? Are those accents supposed to be thumped out literally just as written?

Abby Whiteside writes, "Trying to accent or hold these middle tones (keeping the keys down) complicates the playing without producing any results tangible to the ear." We deduce that these are signals indicating a feeling or a "leaning" in the performance, almost subjective. Above all they telegraph, "Don't forget about me!" The composer's intent would appear not to have us haul off and produce some heart-arresting klunk of the thumbs but to alert us not to obscure the significance of the accented notes in the bass figure.

The essential quality we are after here is not the hard thumb-thumps of contrapuntal insinuation, but rather the linear enrichment of orchestration. We are attempting to play on keys the effect that a cello or woodwind creates in a chamber ensemble. Quite simply, we are "voicing" a part of the piece.

Dominant note. The sound of one note of a chord ("voicing") over the others is described explicitly by Ferguson in his *Piano Music of Six Great Composers*. Encountered frequently, for example, in Beethoven's "Moonlight Sonata," Opus 27, No. 2, in C-sharp minor, and Chopin's previously mentioned Prelude in F-sharp, Opus 28, No. 8, the essence of this seems to be a matter of weight, *not* prior attack. As Ferguson points out, "the marcato note will doubtless sound an instant before the light notes—for even if the fingers strike the keys simultaneously, the key struck with the greater energy will descend more rapidly."

Accents for Learning. As basting thread is used in assembling cloth parts of a piece of sewing, light accents can be applied to dominant beats of the measure to address difficult passage work. Note this example of Beethoven's Sonata in C Major, Opus 2, No. 2, 4th Movement, as follows:

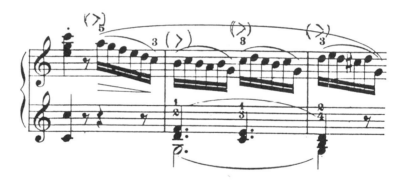

Or Liszt's Concert Etude No. 2:

These slight accents not only stabilize the rhythm but also help to form a pattern for various hand-sets, thus gradually working them into your muscle memory. As you practice further on into the piece, the slight accents, unlike a bad fingering habit, should be simple to subdue and merely pull out like a piece of basting thread.

Memorizing. The very mention of the "m" word finds us cursing Franz Liszt, before whose time it was common to play with the music before one and open on the music rack. William S. Newman reminds us that some of Liszt's critics at the time called the practice of playing without music an affectation.

Samuel Johnson stated that, "The true art of memory is the art of attention." To that Tobias Matthay, who believed that memory builds on what is behind, would have added, "The moment you begin to doubt your memory's capacity thus to 'follow on,' that moment you will hinder, if not completely stop, its continuity of action."

Not surprisingly I am more flexible on this subject. My own experience reveals that certain compositions necessitate (for me) a glimpse at the keyboard now and then to maintain accuracy when dealing with sizable leaps, clusters of block chords, and abrupt key changes. Similarly I seem to need an occasional peek at the music even if it is for no more than a reassuring check on the bass line.

Newman says, "It [man] also permits the music to be called forth from inside oneself. So that the notes are assimilated before rather than *while* they are performed." There you have the tie-in with Matthay's memory-building idea.

This is a good place to remind ourselves that one of our sight-reading tools, the analysis of the harmonic structure we undertook during the initial silent study of a piece, is equally valuable in stimulating memory retention, for if we remember that a section consists of chromatically descending half-cadences or diminished chord inversions, it is easier to bring back the whole of it.

In addition to the total comprehension that memory affords, there is a reward attached to truly learning pieces by heart and making them yours. It is a basic part of playing the piano. While this needn't apply to every piece you learn, it is wise to have part of your repertoire locked up inside your head.

Memory advocates say to remove the music from the rack or the temptation to cheat will become too great, I suppose like taking a shower with a bunch of naked people: it's too hard not to have a look.

Newman says to place the music on top of the piano someplace so that one has to stand up in order to check the notes. Nonsense. Why bother? By taking a page or short section at a time, which is the usual method of committing material to memory, the progress from one session to another can be dramatic. Still, gigantic eons of time will disappear in the process. I, for one, would say that if you are a poor memorizer don't be a purist about it. Feel satisfied in leaving the music open and playing as well as you can. Difficult parts, chiefly because they are repeated during practice sessions, usually find their way into our memories anyway, and much of the rest sticks as well. Don't fight it.

I have good support for this notion from an article in *The Piano Quarterly* (1989) by Anthony Tommasini, pianist and music critic for the *Boston Globe*. He puts into perspective the dictum of not allowing music for performances. He points to the fine teacher and concert pianist Gilbert Kalish of Boston as a man that has a successful musical career and yet persists in having his piano score on the music rack at all times.

Kalish says the "genius of communication [and the] genius of total recall may not occur together." The message is obvious. A great pianist may have difficulty in memorizing well. Moreover, even a great memorizer may lose his ability with the years. "As we grow and develop, we deepen and get more complex in our thinking, and perhaps more neurotic in it. Things we did easily as a youth become harder." Face it.

Indeed, as Tommasini points out, "The brilliant American pianist William Masselos, currently on the faculty at Juilliard, struggled with memory. In his prime he usually chose to play from music. And the British pianist Dame Myra Hess, by any measure one of the most distinguished pianists of her generation, also agonized over her memory insecurities. Hess played almost exclusively from music and was criticized often for doing so." Now come on: isn't that enough good company?

Playing cadenzas. Note technique might seem an unlikely place to include a note on playing these troublesome bits of filigree. However, they occur so frequently in Chopin, Liszt, and elsewhere that they need to be addressed in order to believably render parts of the Nocturnes, Ballades, Etudes, and the rest. It is discouraging to witness the disintegration of an otherwise manageable piece due to a seizing up on the cadenzas. I might liken the phenomenon to the puns that Oliver Wendell Holmes described in *Autocrat at the Breakfast Table:* "People that make puns [read "bad cadenzas"] are like wanton boys that put coppers on the railroad tracks. They amuse themselves and other children, but their little trick may upset a freight train of conversation for the sake of a battered witticism."

Dogged practice and memory work alone will place these soaring extravagances in charge and bring them to heel. Take this example from Chopin's Nocturne in D-flat Major, Opus 27, No. 2:

This is one of the most popular Nocturnes. It is included in numerous anthologies. However, unless you can shift the right hand into a sort of "automatic pilot" mode for these two measures, the whole piece — your whole freight train, so to speak — will be derailed.

In many figures like this, certain logic can generally be found to prevail. Mark the beats with vertical slashes. Number the fingering and group the sequences into phrases. Practice the right hand alone. At the moment of combining the hands you must recall Rodolfo's words near the end of *La Bohème*, "Coraggio!" Employ agogic accents so you can lean on these gravitational centers and find some orientation. Then "aim" toward the note upon which you will finally come to rest as surely as a pirouetting ballerina will terminate her twirl facing the audience. You must instigate a strong magnetic impulse toward the B-flat chord with which the cadenza finishes. The exotic embroidery of the right hand as against the stalwartness of the left could be likened visually to the process of dropping a giant boat anchor to a secure holding and paying out the links of loose chain with the boat floating, bobbing, turning restlessly about on the surface until the chain draws taut. Here we see the feathery flight of one hand brought home by the relentless rhythmic discipline of the other. Unity is ultimately achieved. Oh, and one thing more, breathe.

Pedaling. Almost all writers on this subject caution against laying on the pedal excessively when learning new material. They correctly describe this temptation on two counts; first, to blur the unlearned notes and help to obfuscate the very objective of initial clarity, and second, to freight the performance prematurely with a powerful interpretive element. Both breaches of pedal discipline — as disguise and enrichment — are best put off until later.

While agreeing with the basic idea of restraint in pedaling at the early stages, Ernst Bacon put this problem in delightful perspective when he wrote, "Pedaling should be introduced from the outset of a work's study, and not be added later as a separate ingredient. . . . [I]f the fruit is to be dehydrated, it must first be plucked ripe from the tree. [Lovely!] . . . Now as between pedaling too much or too little, I greatly prefer the former, for it at least allows the piano's normal voice to sound. Better a slightly blurred resonance than an unrelieved dryness." Bacon's words on this occur in his *Notes on the Piano,* and are some of the most intelligent to be found.

To aid you in putting this matter of creative pedaling in perspective, it is best to return to the basic quest for an ideal tone *in the surroundings* in which you find yourself and given the music you are playing. When practicing in the domestic environment in which most of us work, the pedal should generally be used sparingly and only employed to create the sustained effect for which it was intended.

However, this is a rule that needs to be stretched frequently but knowingly in the interest of beauty. I recall seeing a televised performance by Horowitz playing the "Funeral March" from Chopin's B-flat minor Sonata where I could not observe his foot once leave the sustaining pedal nor detect the least lowering of the dampers toward the strings. Undoubtedly the size of the hall, acoustics, and his own fantastic control of tone and volume were sufficient for the purpose.

More recently Paul Badura-Skoda appeared on PBS in a colossal performance of Chopin's B minor Sonata, during which he allowed the Bösendorfer Imperial virtual free rein, come what may. Again the hall was large and the concert well attended.

Beyond the issue of volume, it is worth noting that both pianists, by releasing unrestrained piano tones, were able to draw near orchestral (or, at the very least, organ or harpsichord) sounds from their glorious instruments. Their range of color was greatly expanded. Moreover, certain effects seemed almost delayed in their aural image, as if their contrasting color represented sections of an orchestra that were seated behind or at the side of the dominant melodic source.

What can we learn from this? Recognizing the disadvantages of blurring or merging as a devious misuse of the sustaining pedal, approach resourceful pedaling solely as a device for obtaining specific coloring effects. After the rudiments of a piece are tucked away, try experimenting with over-pedaling for these enlarged orchestral effects. At least enjoy the occasional thrill of unleashing the uncanny generative power of the open strings. Don't be dissuaded from utilizing this worthy tool to employ against the time when your surroundings may permit exploiting the full potential of the undampered piano.

Rubato and agogic accents. These are laudably detailed by Louis Kentner in his book, *Piano.* Rubato—literally a "robbing"—means a value taken away and put back, meaning not just capriciously slowed down. It implies a responsibility to the basic rhythm, not a mere license to let the beat meander all over the map. It's sort of a Robin Hood concept where there is some morality involved, not just perpetual looseness. Kentner wrote, "These are slight leans or prolongations of certain notes (with corresponding acceleration of the non-accented notes) to underline or clarify chord progressions, simple changes and complicated modulations alike."

Note these added agogic accents in Haydn's Sonata in G Major:

Study these fundamentals and incorporate them into your playing. Begin with your silent sight-reading of a piece and immediately start building "bottom up."

Relish these choicest of words by Virgil Thomson in 1940 about practicing: "I've discovered music all over again. And it turns out to be just as it was when I was seventeen, the daily functioning of practicing a beloved instrument and of finding one's whole life filled with order and with energy as a result."

Chapter 8

Repertoire: A Personal Matter

In choosing my ideal repertoire I have taken liberties in several directions. For one thing it is not wholly *my* repertoire; it is my ideal repertoire, that is one I would *like* to play. The fact is that I do practice and play most of it after a fashion. I treat it as if it was my repertoire. So the representation is not completely fraudulent. However, some of the selections are beyond the depth of the intermediate amateur, which I believe myself to be. Still, I find it possible to get through most of these items fairly well and shrug off the missed notes and slow tempi of the remainder as excellent sight-reading and character-building.

Another liberty is in artificially stopping the calendar at this moment of writing which has the effect of immobilizing a limited group of composers and selections as if we had come across them frozen in an ice pack somewhere. Nevertheless, without cheating there seems to be no other way to show a typical, aggressive, large amateur repertoire and discuss its development and maintenance.

I wanted to suggest how an ambitious list of semi-difficult to difficult material, once brought up to a level of a median amateur's competence, might be cultivated. A better heading for this list would probably be "Repertoire and Work in Progress." The plan here is to provide sufficient room for innovation and rotation within the list both to feed the player's enthusiasm and to ward off boredom. Needless to say, it should be revised frequently.

William S. Newman in *The Pianist's Problems* delineates the chief eras of keyboard music — Baroque, Classic, Romantic, and Modern — then writes, "Unless the students are invited into the other three areas, they tend to choose little else but Romantic pieces. They need a more balanced diet, even among the pieces under way at any one time." This very cross-pollination that is available among the periods of piano composition can ensure the health and vigor of your musical raw materials. As one cannot live a healthy life on protein alone, similarly a heavy intake of Romantic sweets is tantamount to taking all of one's meals in a confectioner's shop, though it will be obvious that my own sentiments lie there.

Baroque Music

It would be the saddest of occurrences if an amateur pianist were to regard the playing of Baroque music as if he were choking down large, unpalatable vitamin pills. He need only regard this statement by Charles Rosen in Dennis Matthews's *Keyboard Music*, that Bach's two-part inventions "were explicitly written to foster not a virtuoso technique, but a *singing style* of playing." That should assuage any erstwhile critics of Baroque as being dry and dull and lacking in sentimental appeal. Some appreciation and involvement in early music can be downright life-changing. How many things one encounters in one's educative process can promise that?

Pablo Casals regarded the playing of Bach as the ideal way in which to begin the day, or, for that matter, any practice session. To clear the mind and emotions, what better material is there to place on your music rack than this pure, objective music?

Even though we spoke earlier of changing around the different segments of the practice period, perhaps an exception should be made in the instance of Baroque. Being the most fundamental of music, it does not make emotional demands on the performer, nor call for exaggerated dynamics or tricky pedaling, nor forceful sforzandos or great marathon phrases. It does not ask for rubatos, expressivos, ritardandos, crescendos or diminuendos, or acrobatic scales or key changes. Most of these effects achieved by diacritical markings and Italian phrases applied to romantic music are *written into the notation* of Bach so that the music itself performs them, not the player. It is this literalness that so well suits it to the commencement of our endeavors by helping us to let go of our*selves*.

Domenico Scarlatti

Scarlatti's dates run almost concurrently with Bach's (1685–1750/7). His style is uniquely his own. His prolific output of around six hundred Sonatas is overwhelming. To have some three or four selections of his on hand at all times is an excellent reinforcement for the more central baroque thrust of Bach. Humor and catchy invention in the main melody line are his strong points. He strikes me as the Haydn and Schubert of his era. Do not look for the almost mathematical balancing of voices and ideas and the tapestry-like stitchery of Bach. Scarlatti thinks in a single, vital line in a direct and unique manner.

Scarlatti spent much time in Spain and displays some of the Spanish folk sound in his Sonatas, as does Chopin in his Preludes and somewhat in his Nocturnes. Accordingly, he exerted influence on some Spanish composers like Albéniz and Granados.

Johann Sebastian Bach

Dennis Matthews had this story to tell about Brahms. "When [Wagner] and Brahms were being entertained at Koblenz by a certain Councillor Wegler, a rare bottle of Rauenthaler was produced and sampled. Their host likened its excellence among wines to Brahms among composers, whereupon Brahms immediately called for a bottle of Bach."

Albert Lockwood in his comprehensive, if dated, *Notes on the Literature of the Piano*, paraphrased an old proverb in this way, "A fugue a day keeps bad taste away." He went on to say that "no one for whom the music of Bach has meaning and beauty needs to distrust his taste in other composers."

This music is still fundamentally polyphonic and bears that style's hallmarks of evenness in voicing and regularity of rhythm. Put another way, a single voice does not dominate throughout nor do pulsating dynamic or rhythmic surges occur as they might in romantic music.

Although Bach can on occasion sound richly romantic, as in the Prelude in G-flat minor, Book 2 of the "Well-Tempered Clavier" (WTC), or the first movement of the sixth Partita. He can, if you choose, be made more so by emphasizing or forcing a cantabile singing style beyond the printed notation. This emotional content, though present in the subtle apprehension and perceptions of the listener, is best conveyed by the music itself and a controlled, thoughtful performance.

Some of the very best advice for playing Bach is given by Donald Tovey in his preface to Book 2 of the "Well-Tempered Clavier." With respect to part playing (polyphony) he writes, "No part needs 'bringing out' at the expense of the others, but on the pianoforte care is most needed for that part which is more in danger of *failure of tone*." Then, "The pianoforte player will manage it when he can give a good account of Chopin's Prelude in E-minor[!]."

Surely we have an abundance of evidence of the value of Bach. André Previn once told me years ago, "When I have progressed through a variety of musical careers (which indeed he has) and have had the good luck to reach the advanced age of eighty, I will retire to my studio and play only Bach."

Charles Rosen writes that Beethoven made his reputation as a young boy by playing (what else?) the "Well-Tempered Clavier."

Clara Schumann as a young girl, on Christmas morning, decided to bestow the ultimate gift upon her father, Robert. She performed for him the entire forty-eight Preludes and Fugues from memory. What a glorious gift.

Joseph Hofmann, the legendary pianist, when asked if Bach's music is particularly useful in developing a good technique said, "Bach's music is particularly qualified to develop the fingers in conjunction with music expression and thematic characterization.... that some of his music seems dry ... think yourself into his style, and you will find a mine of never dreamed enjoyment."

Huneker states that "Before playing a concert [Chopin] shut himself up and played, not Chopin, but Bach, always Bach. Absolute finger independence and touch discrimination and color are to be gained by playing the Preludes and Fugues of Bach."

Well, do I hear a cry of "Uncle!"?

The realistic Donald Tovey mercifully suggests that perfection of the ornaments be eliminated in the beginning. Obviously this is to aid the flow of notes and remove potential stumbling blocks. He further advocates that hands be practiced separately to aid listening for the inner voices, and to understand and feel the melodic surges.

Throughout the study of Bach there are accepted conventions applicable to the various patterns of notes:

• In general, a flowing or legato series of notes in one hand is offset by either staccato or portamento effects in the other.

• A majority of short themes occurring in either hand terminate on the first and third beats.

• The numbers 2, 3, 4, and 5 near the signature refer to the number of voices or parts of the fugue. Your study of this form can be greatly aided by highlighting the entry of the various voices with a marking pen.

• The expression "Let in the air" is attributed to Tausig and describes a method of relieving tension, letting the music breathe, relaxing as much as possible. A formidable fugue such as the A minor in Book 1 of WTC may seem a little easier and more approachable with that phrase borne in mind.

• Use the pedal sparingly in Bach. This does not mean not to use it at all. Keep it restricted to its fundamental use of holding notes, not as a device for blurring notes and creating expression so that the fine value of the individual voices is destroyed. A little pedal is just fine. Bach would surely have used it if it had been available to him.

• Do not pounce on the themes as they enter like a dog on raw hamburger. Think more of voicing than announcing.

• Lead *into* the first and third beats, terminating these with a very light accent.

• If a note is to be held for a long time, give it a little muscle in taking it down so the sound will last. Such a warning was not needed for the plucked notes of the undampered harpsichord.

• All of Bach is worth turning over constantly in your schedule. While no specific sequence is mandatory, here is a suggested one:

	Number of pieces
Two-Part Inventions	15
Three-Part Inventions (Sinfonia)	15
Well-Tempered Clavier	48
English Suites	6
French Suites	6
Partitas (German Suites)	6
Chromatic Fantasia and Fugue	
A-minor Fugue	
Toccatas	7
Italian Concerto	

Keep these in perpetual rotation. Indulge in numerous repeats. Play them again and again. If the Preludes and Fugues in seven sharps or flats cause too much anguish and prevent you from even getting out of the starting gate, do not let them thwart you with respect to the whole set. Just skip over them and do not look back. After all, there are over one hundred fine pieces just listed, and we have not depleted the Baroque period *or even Bach* as yet.

Still, it is worthwhile to say that a lifetime devotion to this subject — even fifteen minutes of your practice time daily — will find you slowly but surely raising your level of play for these and all your other works.

Random notes influence me to mention that Invention No. 8 in F is a favorite of TV commentator Edwin R. Newman. WTC Fugue was beloved by Schweitzer who often played it on his upright in the wilds of Africa. William F. Buckley greatly admires his friend Rosalyn Tureck's playing of "one of the most beautiful pieces ever written," the first movement of the sixth Partita. Certainly not least is my own suspicion that the delightful thematic air from Toccata No. 1, second Fugue, made its own minor contribution to "Let the Sunshine In," from the popular rock musical *Hair*.

For those who simply must have some exercises or perish, unfold any of the first movements or concluding Gigues of the Bach Suites and look no further.

The Classical Period and Transition

Joseph Haydn

The Sonatas of Haydn are truly enjoyable. Albert Lockwood makes the statement, "The only work of Haydn the pianist need study is the Variation in F-minor, which is certainly his most important work; it is effective in recitals. The sonatas have charm in spots, but only a specialist would care to play many of them." Such curt dismissal is unworthy of this former great teacher and performer. The humor and inventiveness of Haydn are a delightful contrast to the dominant composer for the piano of this period, Mozart; in fact a bit like Scarlatti was to Bach—that is they seem to contain a mischievous quality plus that rare ingredient, humor.

It is heartrending to read this composer's tragic life, but doing so makes his work more comprehensible. Hutcheson concludes his descriptions of Haydn's Sonatas by saying, "The sweetness of the man's nature is reflected in his lightest creations. When he adds depth of thought to charm he is truly great, and he was not unlike most later composers in customarily putting his weightier ideas into his first movements or into his Adagios and Andantes." Certainly this was true in the Sonatas of both Beethoven and Chopin.

The numbering of Haydn Sonatas is not always uniform, since it sometimes follows the whim of the publishers. It is for that reason that I wish to set forth the actual first measures of works that should be of appeal to amateurs such as myself:

As for permanent inclusion in the repertoire, it might be best to gulp down Lockwood's crabbed advice and limit oneself to the Variations in F minor, a truly great and popular work. This is a superior piece of music that is often heard in concerts, yet quite accessible to the amateur. Then add the two-part Sonatas in G and E minor (see above).

Mozart

With several excellent Sonatas to choose from, why not select some of the most beautiful, advanced and complex of those and keep them in rotation rather than spread your efforts too thinly over this consummate composer? No one is prepared to deny the beauty, charm, facile musicality, and wizardry of Mozart, but there are bigger fish to fry, so to speak. Man's span being "but three score and ten," we need to limit our endeavors in the classical period unless it is the pianist's wish to specialize.

These are the recommended Sonatas:

Fanatasia in C minor	K. 475
Sonata in C minor (usually played with above)	K. 457
Sonata in A minor	K. 310
Sonata in D Major	K. 284
Sonata in A Major	K. 331
Rondo in A minor	K. 511

Quibble if you care, but I ask only that whatever you tamper with, make the list shorter than longer: I have already listed too many for a balanced repertoire.

Note that there is *only* one Sonata in a minor key, the A minor, which in addition to its inherent beauty and dramaturgy, might be a tie-breaking reason to include it. It was said to have been written after the death of Mozart's mother. Successful performances of this work seem to start right off with a rather angry insistence, perhaps the composer's own agony over his loss. Things progress in the first movement development to some advanced demands on both hands that must operate together but diversely. At times of such frantic ambivalence a good rule is to take yourself by the scruff of the neck and focus attention on one hand or the other (usually the left), thus absolutely forcing the remaining one to accompany. This focusing device is made easier by a familiarity with baroque polyphonic music. Otherwise, trying to divide attention absolutely equally customarily results in a sort of keyboard gridlock where things come to a grinding, cataclysmic halt.

The question will come up here as with Beethoven, at least up to the later Sonatas, as to whether time should be spent on playing slow movements through in their entirety. Despite the time involved, the arguments flow strongly in favor of doing so. The philosophy seems to be, "If not now, when?" These adagios, largos, and andantes help the player assimilate the whole work and prepare him for rendering compositions and not fragments. Technically they can be more difficult than some rapid tempo movements, at least in establishing a mood and maintaining a steady rhythm.

An added cause of trouble in slow passages occurs in the case of cadenzas and leisurely paced ornaments. Such rapid note passages demand meticulous rehearsal, preferably with a metronome. In the case of cadenzas, mark the major beats with vertical slashes. Notate any ornaments by ballooned enlargements above or out in the side margin. Then set the metronome at half speed, draw your lips into a thin blue line, and proceed. There is no better preparation for encountering the same trouble spots in Chopin's Nocturnes.

Franz Schubert

To overlook Schubert is not to know and appreciate one of the most creative of all melodists. In his classic, *Notes on the Literature of the Piano,* Albert Lockwood writes on this point when he says, "His brain seethed unceasingly with melodies which were left on the town, as it were, without education. Witness the thousands of themes."

It has been said that in listening to Schubert, we forget the instrument being played at the moment and are conscious only of pure music — an amazing quality.

Donald Ferguson offers this wonderful thought about Schubert, "For the true amateur, the true music lover, there is a special corner of the mind in which, like keepsakes and other mementos of precious moments, he stores up the piano pieces of Franz Schubert." There was an astonishing originality buzzing in Schubert's head. His enharmonic chord changes — that is, making instant modulations based on one or two notes in common — were a major compositional advance from the period in which he was writing.

We can identify such caprices in the works of Scarlatti, Haydn, and Schubert as genuine lightheartedness. In contradistinction, the movements of Beethoven and Schumann, labeled "Mit Humor," come across with all the hilarity of an exploding cigar. The fancifulness of Scarlatti, Haydn, and Schubert does not seem to surface in a major composer again until Debussy when it is manifest more in an aura of irony.

The group of piano pieces known as Opus 90 is an excellent repertoire staple. It is popular, featured occasionally in concerts, listenable, and fun to play. It possesses great variety and addresses several technical areas. No. 1 is a warm-up for those jarring dotted rhythms that later plague Schumann's finales and marches (should you ever be obsessed with learning one of those) and is a good all-around test for control of bombast. No. 2 is excellent for practice in passage work that will forever free you of the need for drilling the E-flat Major scale. No. 3, over-popular as it is, is still a nice challenge in sustained control of a thumbed melody. The bass figures can be excitingly developed later on. Phrasing is vital here, and the strong, sweet melody is a corker and a good bet to make voices husky and eyes damp. No. 4 is a textbook example of hand/wrist rotation exploited to the fullest. What frivolity and lightness it expresses!

The Theme and Variations of Opus 142, No. 4, in B-flat, stand sufficiently independently to work nicely as a separate, impressive piece. These variations are lovely: include them in your regular schedule. They are not long but cover a good range of problems in an atmosphere of great beauty. This commitment will slake any thirst you may have to practice the B-flat Major scale.

The small A Major Sonata, Opus 120, is a delight. I won't bet eating my hat on it, but if you can play the third movement without realizing where "Send in the Clowns" originated, it will certainly fly off my head. The great B-flat Major Sonata is worth some study, not so much because of note difficulty, but is one more challenge for containment, that is shaping a lengthy work and holding it all together. To these two Sonatas mentioned above, the dependable Opus 143 in A minor would also be a good addition. In his book, *Piano Music of Six Great Composers,* Donald N. Ferguson includes Schubert along with Beethoven, Schumann, Chopin, Brahms, and Debussy, to which I would only add Liszt and drop no one.

Perhaps inspired by Schubert's own adventurousness with keys, a short digression on key signature might be permitted in order to ventilate some ideas. Anyone who has suffered through the growing pains of student pop bands and had a gift of even relative pitch has heard enough B-flats to last him a lifetime. Trumpets, trombones, most saxophones, and clarinets are pitched in B-flat "concert," meaning that if the piano plays B-flat they can enjoy their most rudimentary finger pattern: octaves, fifths, and higher thirds and sevenths can occur in the "open" positions without using valves.

It is, therefore, not surprising that these tyros lean on the simple "flat" keys of F, B-flat, and E-flat to make it easier for them to manipulate their instruments. Somehow my prejudice against these keys has lasted up to this day when I still have trouble finding them fascinating. In a way it may relate to string players who traditionally avoid sustaining bowed notes on their open strings of G, D, A, and E, because they will sound dead—there being no way to alter pitch or produce a vibrato.

I only mention this to bring to light not only the prejudices and predilections that performers can feel toward keys, but to suggest, as is sometimes written, that the same is true of composers. Certain keys not only articulate differently, but they even speak and resonate differently. Some trigger special emotional responses, believe it or not. Just as F, B-flat, and E-flat induce boredom in me, so E Major seems warm and A-flat and B Major unaccountably beckoning and cozy.

Ludwig Van Beethoven

The trinity of his three writing periods is important, since we will constantly shift our allegiances, dipping in impartially at times, at others making a fetish of as much as we can comprehend of the abstruseness of the last great Sonatas. In doing so we can strive for representative Sonatas from all the periods including choices of reasonable accessibility at the easy end, and, at the hard end, obviously omitting the ominous Hammerklavier. Though this might be readable by certain top-level amateurs it probably is not playable just because of the improbability of holding so much together and making it sound believable, *even if* the notes were all played correctly.

I like this list. While only including a third of the Sonatas, it cuts across the three periods and employs a diversity of keys, moods, and popularity:

Period	Work	Key
Early	Opus 2 No. 2	A Major
	Opus 2 No. 3	C Major
	Opus 7	E-flat Major
	Opus 13 ("Pathetique")	C minor
Middle	Opus 22	B-flat Major
	Opus 27 No. 2 ("Moonlight")	C-sharp minor
	Opus 31 No. 2 ("Tempest")	D minor
Late	Opus 57 ("Appassionata")	F minor
	Opus 90	E minor
	Opus 109	E Major
	Opus 111	C minor

This last has the "jazz variations" near the end, which are great fun to try, especially if you have an ear for that kind of thing. Moreover, Tovey says that, although difficult, the Sonata responds to routine practice, and I found this more or less true, whereas most of us could practice the Hammerklavier night and day and fail to raise it above the most plodding level.

Romantic

Frederick Chopin

Itzhak Perlman said during one of his White House concerts, where he was sharing the stage with a fine young pianist, "It is too bad that we violinists do not have a Chopin."

True. What a giant! If cast away on the legendary desert island with any old, prewar Steinway B in good operating condition, and limited to three composers and one category of each's work, the probable triumvirate should be Bach's "Well-Tempered Clavier," Beethoven's Sonatas, and Chopin's Etudes. Well, I would have felt shortchanged on the Chopin since Etudes are Etudes, and I might have argued forcibly that the Preludes should be included as well and, ah, maybe the Nocturnes in trade for some early Fugues because, after all, it was a desert island and one needs something more aesthetically satisfying after all the work is done.

So let there be the Etudes, and let there be the Preludes. But could we depart without the ballades, the Polonaise-Fantasie, the Fantasie in F minor, the two Sonatas, Nocturnes, Scherzi, and Impromptus? What a fantastic legacy we have been left: a new way of playing the piano, the Etudes all written out to show us how to do it, a wealth of additional material, with dances and songs shimmering over it all, a profusion of everlasting beauty.

Etudes. The technical advances ushered in by Chopin are what caused me to agree with the others that advocate the daily commitment to practicing the Etudes. Warm up on the Baroque music, if time allows. Then consider playing most of the Etudes from Opus 10 one day, and those from Opus 25 the next, alternating right on from there for the rest of your life.

Marthe Morhange-Motchane, in her *Thematic Guide to Piano Literature*, ranks the "Etude in Thirds," Opus 25, No. 6, along with seven others in her most advanced category. I place it in the virtuoso

category and am still back at the slow metronome stage after two
years of working at it. This work would have come a lot easier if I
had begun drilling double thirds very early in my endeavors, as
brought up earlier in chapter seven. Like hitting bull's-eyes in the
dark, this type of coordination may require a gift of skill at birth, but
the practice is good discipline anyway. So, just like facing a trip to
the dentist, keep working on double thirds: they are simply employed too often to shirk. To show in what respect they are held, in
competition among aspiring concert pianists the contestants are
often prohibited from warming up with double thirds lest a display
of that unique show-off talent unduly influences the judges.

Preludes. Be aware that some performers play these as an entire performance group. Louis Kentner breaks after the ravishing
No. 8 then goes right through to the end. No. 16 is another virtuoso
piece that takes a lot of slow practice with the metronome, being
perhaps only a notch less difficult than the Etude in Thirds. For the
frolicsome, this prelude can also be practiced for fun and possible
benefit in a jazz rhythm by improvising accents on the off beats. It
has a most modern sound this way. Try it at a nice, solid medium
tempo. No. 24 has those dangerous thirds built into its tension-
packed climax, the difficulty of which can be lessened by adopting
a ritardando on the three notes preceding the descent by thirds, then
commencing the cascade slowly and picking up speed until the previous established tempo is resumed: that durable rubato device of
stealing and giving back. I practice 3, 5, *8*, 10, *12*, *16*, 18, 19, 23, *24*,
and 25 (or at least the cadenza). Morhange-Motchane grades the
italicized ones as the most advanced, and I certainly concur.

Sonatas. These two grand works should be playable by the
committed amateur. I would lean toward the third only because of
its greater homogeneity. Its lines are longer in all movements except
the second. You have the possibility of working toward an inclusive
mood in this work, which is impossible to say about the second
Sonata, regardless of its spectacularly rich first movement and great
Scherzo and funeral march. Still, as Schumann said of Chopin, "[he]
bound together four of his maddest children." This is to say (here in
the words of James Huneker, who is your man when it comes to studying Chopin), "These four movements have no common life."
    The first movements of both Sonatas require extensive work.

After some diligence they should be accessible as should the entire works. The Pollini CD combining the two is a great working tool and as good as any text there is.

Nocturnes. Over the ages these have proven to be, next to the "Well-Tempered Clavier" and Beethoven's Sonatas, one of the most published of piano works. Of these there is a group that a brief scanning of recorded collections will reveal to be the most popular which, in one way of speaking, means they are probably the most beautiful to the most people. They are:

Opus 15 Nos. 1, 2, and 3
Opus 27 No. 1
Opus 32 No. 1
Opus 37 Nos. 1 and 2
Opus 48 Nos. 1 and 2
Opus 55 No. 1
Opus 62 No. 2
Opus 72 No. 1

To keep the continuity of this group you can merely write the page number of the next selection at the very end of the one before in those instances where others intervene.

Scherzos. Representing some of his latest work, these show Chopin's most sophisticated style. The first is a tiger to learn but, as Charles Cooke points out, will repay a painstaking metronomic base. Since so much is repeated, good early groundwork bears a fine harvest. The second is justifiably popular and affords a good chance to show off some major league cantabile playing in your three times through the main theme and two times through the trio. Again, there is a bountiful crop in the offing if you prepare carefully.

Mazurkas. The musicality of these folk songs creeps up on you to the point where you suddenly shout out, "These are great piano pieces!" They seem so simple and unaffected, almost like popular sheet music, that you are apt to be deceived. Then you encounter the beauty that lies within them, even one so simple that Michael Cimino used it in *The Deerhunter* as the haunting tune played by the drinking buddies in the Philadelphia bar from which he traumatically cut to the horror of Vietnam. This little list of mazurkas forms a fine program when performed as a group:

Opus 7 No. 1   Opus 59 Nos. 2 and 3
Opus 17 No. 4   Opus 63 No. 3
Opus 24 No. 4   Opus 67 Nos. 3 and 4
Opus 33 Nos. 2 and 4   Opus 68 No. 4

Ballades. This group of four masterpieces forms the crown jewel of Chopin's artistic maturity. Start with the code of No. 4 and work backward. Your greatest challenge will be to keep them unified.

Mendelssohn

This underplayed composer created some beguiling shorter works which one should have handy. Some say of him, "No feeling, no heart." These selections disprove that. The "Songs without Words" are lovely pieces of music. The most beautiful seem popular with everyone. They are a joy to play and a joy to hear. This is borne out by the frequency of recording as evidenced by a cross-referencing of several collections on disc, plus my own sentiments while practicing them. These also form a nice program when done this way.

Opus 19 Nos. 1 and 2
Opus 30 No. 6
Opus 38 No. 6
Opus 53 Nos. 1*, 2, and 3
Opus 62 No. 6
Opus 67 Nos. 4 and 6

*I am ready to eat my hat again if you do not hear Simon and Garfunkel's "Bridge Over Troubled Waters" emerge from the theme of this piece.

The Barenboim CD of these is excellent, and Moriz Rosenthal recorded most of these same selections. Try to restrain a snicker when you recognize "The Spring Song" as one of my choices. Your job is to overcome whatever triteness might be bred of its vaudeville use as a staple to accompnay an inept comic dancer and to transcend such crass associations with its lovely beguiling melody and deep sonorities of its harmonies.

Good exercise is Mendelssohn's cheery warhorse, "Rondo

Capriccioso." Like "Spinnerleid," it calls for a tight seatbelt and lock-jaw rhythm. The payoff is a marvelous roller-coaster ride of fun.

To add to the variations repertoire, "Variations Serieuses," Opus 54, is a superior composition that is at once difficult and accessible and quite attractive both for the player and his audience. Likewise, the first "Prelude and Fugue," Opus 35, No. 1, is worth a continuing major effort. It should remain a permanent repertoire candidate. For a pianist casting sheep's eyes in the direction of César Franck's awesome "Prelude, Chorale and Fugue," this, along with Fugues of Bach, is a mandatory starting place. It embodies a basic fugal concept plus the silky, seamless, melting effect of late romantic fugue metaphors. Even less profound than the above are two measurable pieces from his Miscellaneous Compositions, No. 1 of "Trois Caprices," Opus 33, and "Andante Cantabile e Presto Agitato." These are found in Schirmer's output. They have marked similarity in being pattern pieces that, once learned, enable the amateur to scream ahead like a bat out of hell: sheer fun they are.

Schumann

Failing to see much connection with the rest of his work, I put the Toccata in a special category. It deserves its own shrine and its separate novenas in the practice repertoire. It deserves its own metronome setting and all else you can give it. Once you know the notes, it demands at least twice weekly airing, and much more if it is to be raised to a performance level. Tempo should be set well below where frequent errors are made, and yet it should be kept listenable. Maintain the second- and fourth-beat sforzandos religiously, and pray a great deal. Try for a nice lilting effect on the held notes that start the descending pattern before the coda. Once when Leschetizky was talking about various pianists who did not play the Toccata, he added, "Of course they've *all* studied it."

Lockwood bestows praise grudgingly on Schumann but tends to be behind current piano trends in appreciation. He admits only the Davidsbundlertanzen, Kreisleriana, Fantaisie in C, and Phantasiestücke into the charmed circle. Friskin, writing much later, devotes as much space to Schumann as Beethoven, with the most naturally going to Chopin. I believe most Schumann is accessible, except possibly the Phantasiestücke.

Because this composer rewrites himself so often, it would be reasonable to try to elevate a fair number of his works to repertoire status and keep them in constant rotation. To this end I suggest:

Kreisleriana   Humoresque
Davidsbundlertanzen   Papillons
Phantasiestücke   Scenes from Childhood
Carnaval   Sonata in G minor
Toccata

Garrick Ohlsson in David Dubal's *Reflections from the Keyboard*, complains justifiably about Schumann's dotted rhythms in the finales of several of the pieces above. There is something alienating and a bit passé about that jolting, jarring, bombastic effect that makes me dread spending time on it, almost as if I resisted such destructive treatment of the fragile keyboard. One trick you can try in order to emasculate these percussive thrusts is to drain off sufficient marcato bravado to muffle and suppress the militant quality. Try affecting an almost secretive tension, a sort of conspiratorial whispering up to the point of the various crescendi or sforzandos, following which you can slink back to a stealthy murmur.

Schumann wrote lovely, pianistic, nostalgic melodies. He is seldom awkward, something not often said of Brahms or Beethoven, for example. Mischa Dichter in the Mach book called him the only nineteenth-century composer writing for the twentieth century. Lockwood, he of niggardly praise, called him "German pure."

Franz Liszt

The glory of Liszt and his value to the pianist are harder to define standing next to the bounty of Chopin than they might otherwise be. Liszt combined so many entities other than a composer— man of the world, extrovert, hypnotic performer, creator of choral and orchestral works, philanthropist, teacher without equal, mystic, and harbinger of modern impressionism in music. Excelling as he did in so many areas it is astonishing that he remains at the pinnacle of great composers and rivals the best, most versatile, and most prolific of them.

Do not be chagrined by the glut of black ink and accidentals on page after page of some of his works. Liszt's later style, particularly, demands those trembling block chords and mass chromatic movements which simply beg for lots of sixteenth- and thirty-second-note multiple connecting tails and bee-swarms of sharps, flats, and double accidentals. The hyperbolic, programmatic content of the music simply dictates that type of dense notation as in the Opera Transcriptions, and once you pinpoint the melody and identify the harmonies you can usually figure out what he's cooking up and see your way out of the mess. This resembles what you will do later when confronted with the similarly frustrating configurations of Debussy and Ravel. While admittedly hard to read when coming from a dead start, the persistent amateur pianist-cum-sleuth will find that many of those vibrating chord clusters will sort themselves out with patience and dissection, not to mention dutiful marking of the chords and calm, slow practice. A specific case in point is the first movement of Liszt's Paganini Etudes which your ear will ultimately decipher as one gigantic series of chord tremulos.

Liszt's works that appeal to me most are:

Three Concert Etudes	Hungarian Dances 11 and 12
Mephisto Waltz	Waldesrauschen
Funerailles	Valse Oubliee
Sonata in B minor	Liebesträume
Paganini Etudes	Tristan and Isolde (Trans.)

Brahms

After hearing the Paganini Variations so many years ago in that adjacent apartment in Paris, I just had to have a crack at both books of that masterpiece. Make no mistake about it, the overall work is another of those magnum opus jobs, a true virtuoso piece. For the intermediate amateur to attempt to play it is an impertinence. The hardest variations are in Book 1, being Nos. 1, 2, and 13; and in Book 2, Nos. 1 and 7. Still, even these parts are not totally unapproachable and will at least pose one of the ultimate challenges you may confront at the keyboard. Good, positive accents at the beginnings of measures are a must, firm rhythm as usual, and a light, bouncy style will help. Easy does it as to speed. Nobody is going to tear up your record contract if you play it slowly. Just respect what Jorge Bolet said about the relationship of a steady tempo to listening to a piano played at a distance: the phenomenon of a greater distance imparts a feeling of speed, believe it or not.

For repertoire candidates I propose the following:

• Paganini Variations, which, though they require the most courage, are at the very least worth keeping in an active role.

- Opus 76 All pieces with special attention to 1, 2, 5, and 8
- Opus 117 Nos. 1 and 2
- Opus 118 Nos. 1 and 2, remembering that No. 2 is the lovely intermezzo that influenced me so long ago in Paris
- Opus 79 The Two Rhapsodies.

Rachmaninoff

The Preludes are worthy of any pianist's familiarity. Opus 23, No. 6, which Friskin dubs "a little sweet," is a gush of captivating emotion that demands some first class passage work in the left hand. It is a delight to perform and to listen to as I used to when Oscar Levant played it so lushly. No. 4 in D Major might be considered a trifle insipid by some but embodies some of the No. 6 characteristics and has a healthy romantic climax.

The Prelude in G minor, No. 5, is the most famous of the group and contains the gorgeous middle section that is familiar to all music lovers. The G-sharp minor of Opus 32 is a sophisticated, refined work that is often on concert programs and important to any repertoire. Last, the separately published C-sharp minor, while being in the warhorse category, is well known and loved for good reason. It, too, has a ravishing midsection and will benefit from being played much quieter than is commonly conceived.

On the subject of performing familiar works like the C-sharp minor of Rachmaninoff, the Fantasie-Impromptu, A Major Prelude, E-flat Nocturne of Chopin, "Spring Song," of Mendelssohn, "Für Elise" of Beethoven, and so many others, do not hang back because someone calls them trite. They may be considered trite because of frequent, dull performances, but people love these pieces. The music is there. Just remember Horowitz encoring all the time with "Träumerai." Treat them as if you were Horowitz and could do no wrong. Dig deeply to find the true reason for their enduring popularity. Disregard the label of triteness and reinvent your own perfect understanding of the original composition.

Miscellaneous

The César Franck "Prelude, Chorale, and Fugue" is another successful attempt, like Liszt's, to discover a new, more inventive form for the traditional Sonata but still provide a suggestion of the basic movements as in the case of the late Beethoven Sonatas, Chopin Sonatas in B-flat minor and B minor and the Liszt B minor Sonata. The Franck is another of those works that is tricky to hold together. Its lines are very extended and require great restraint at the outset, monumental rhythmic conviction, and attentive phrasing. The performer must orchestrate and voice throughout, choosing as Franck himself did between organ, orchestra, and piano for the desired effects, yet somehow sustaining everything and ending nothing. He must carry along all this freight on his shoulders and pick up more along the way, balancing and enhancing it.

It is a grand piece with a thrilling climax. If it seems overwhelming at first, stay with it and know that it is a superb, world-class number to keep always in an active performance role. Slow practice not only pays off but sounds wonderful. The player's objective is striving for a cathedral-filling effect.

Scriabin's Etude in D-sharp minor is another Horowitz staple. Talk about a tough left hand to control; if you will, this work employs what Ruth Laredo, a consummate practitioner of material of this stripe, calls a murderous bass. It will be easier if you play some of the high left-hand notes with the right-hand thumb. It is salutary, like a trip to the gym in hot weather. Grit your teeth. Give it a try.

Modern Period

Debussy

This most important composer of the modern era is essential to absorb in some measure. There are several pieces or groups of pieces by Debussy that are strong potentials for consistent work. Speaking of the Preludes, Hutcheson says, "We see in him an acute observer of life and nature rather than an active participator in human drama or emotion." Try

Reflets dans l'Eau
Suite Bergamesque   Deux Arabesques
Le Plus que Lente   Children's Corner

These should all be easily accessible to the amateur. "Reflets dans l'Eau" is a serious concert piece and probably the most valuable mentioned here. Employ strong rhythmic pulses in the second and fourth notes of "Suite Bergamesque," and strive for a melodic sequence of descending thirds in measures when you strike the two accented A's and follow them with the strong F. The same goes for the similar sequence in later bars.

The Preludes are vital cornerstones of modern piano music. Start right out with the first one and make it sound big as a house, round and full. Read as many as you can and keep it up. You will soon get used to the ninth chords with the flatted fifths, the pairing of motifs, and the rest of the trappings.

Ravel

Often spoken of in the same breath as Debussy, this is the second modern composer who should absorb your time quite without consideration of others. The prime pieces with which to concern yourself are:

Sonatine	Pavane for a Dead Infant
Valses Nobles et Sentimentales	Minuet (Haydn)
La Valse (see Transcriptions)	Jeux d'eau

Friskin calls for delicacy rather than power in the first difficult and very dissonant of the Waltzes. This is also one of those rare cases when you cannot concentrate on one hand over the other. While you might lean to the left, as always, you simply must get these harmonies in your head and then take chance. It becomes a lively exercise in what you have already accomplished if, after some days of practice, you put everything you have on automatic pilot and let fly as best you can. Perhaps a comparison with your first sensation of balance on a two-wheel bicycle might be appropriate. Hauling off on these cacophonous chords is akin to being shoved down an incline with the kiddie-wheels removed for the first time. You suddenly realize that no steadying hand is ensuring your balance. It is absolutely amazing not how many wrong notes you will hit but *how many right ones.*

Ferenc Mompou

Try to find and order his "Scènes des Enfants." Oscar Levant used to play this repeatedly and lovingly on his show. He well knew how to bowl over an audience. He would milk that last, bittersweet movement for all it was worth.

Granados

His "Lover and the Nightingale" from Goyescas is worth taking to bed with you. Alicia de Laroccha's recording of this should convince you. Some cross-pollination is discernible between this and Chopin's last E minor Nocturne, perhaps just due to his Spanish sojourn. Rich voicing and steady rhythm are called for.

Unlocking a Composer

By means of listening to recorded works and reading about piano literature, try to develop a sensitivity for those compositions which set you ablaze. Time spent in zeroing in on personally exciting material will have a "domino effect" as far as knocking over the composer's other works.

For example, consider Schumann's Papillons, Opus 2, which may not be regarded as the zenith of Schumann's powers. A thorough exploration of this work will unlock almost everything else he wrote during his creative life. Beginning with the lush octave-filled curtain-raiser, to the alternation of captivating melodies with martial bombast common to his tug-of-war between his ideological Florestan and Eusebius, the style becomes evident. Sure enough, there is even a sampling of the militaristic finale—the pompous dotted rhythms that often concluded his longer works. Here in Papillons everything is in microcosm and encapsulated in an amiable setting.

The usefulness of familiarizing oneself with such a representative work by any composer is to unlock, at least partially, all that can follow. Papillons is more revelatory than usual of early Schumann, but we can do this with all composers. If pushed to name starter pieces with respect to composers' ultimate styles I might state these:

Mozart	Sonata in F Major, K. 332
Schubert	Opus 90, all four movements
Beethoven	Sonata in B-flat, Opus 22
Schubert	Sonata in A Major, Opus 142
Mendelssohn	Songs without Words (selected)
Chopin	Misc. Nocturnes, Opus 9, No. 1
Schumann	Papillons
Liszt	Liebesträume
Brahms	Intermezzos, Opus 118, 1 and 2

Note that all are considered comparatively easy but have been chosen for their characteristic quality.

Transcriptions

William S. Newman writes, "The many transcriptions that Bach himself made are good enough precedents for the use of transcriptions. There is no justification, therefore, for blackballing transcriptions as a class, as is done by some purists. The real criteria must always be the quality of the original, the skill of the transcribing, and the adaptability of the new idiom."

Ravel's "La Valse" makes an excellent case in point since it was not written as a piano piece like "Valses Nobles et Sentimentales," but was transcribed by Ravel *after* the orchestra composition had been made. That is one reason why it is often left out of Ravel's piano selections and occasionally reviled. Another could be that some of the orchestral simulations are simply not pianistic. Still, this is a handsome production with some beguiling melodies and intricate harmonies and modulations. It highlights an aspect of piano performance that affords good study and good fun: that of actually imitating sounds of an orchestra on the piano in a most challenging and sometimes improbable way.

Liszt's transcription of Wagner's "Liebestode" from *Tristan and Isolde* is a sure winner. First of all you have brevity, an asset with which few can quarrel. Next you receive an efficacious dose of Liszt's later dramatic piano style, replete with trembling chords, subtle moving harmonies, bee-swarms of accidentals, and ink-clouds of Art Tatum cadenzas, all of which should set you up for the Paganini Etudes, Gnomenreigen, Funerailles, and many more. Next, you get a surefire climax that will bring down the house as surely as "Vesti La Giubba," and the last eight bars of "When Irish Eyes Are Smiling." If that were not enough, you are blessed with a merciful unwinding of the whole thing by way of a well-constructed denouement or coda.

Gustav Mahler produced little published piano music, but the soulful Adagietto from his Fifth Symphony is available from C.F. Peters Publishing. What a revelation it is to sit at the solo piano and thrill to that special voicing of Mahler's that is so searching and so achingly beautiful. It is not only good "orchestrating" or voicing practice to study it, but a nostalgic look backward to the main title of Visconti's film, *Death in Venice*, where it provided the background and so aptly set the stage and mood for the entire film. It is guaranteed to draw a pleasant response. The notes are not hard to play but remain niggardly in their willingness to sound like sostenuto violins, half of which are bowing long, whole notes and the other half plucking little pizzicatos with punctilious spacing. Rich fun is to be had here. It may cause fainting.

Another good transcription is Samuel Barber's "Adagio for Strings." This is a rounded, seductive, soaring, romantic elegy along the lines of Mahler but lacking his unique, thematic trademark of the descending fourth and orchestral voicing.

In its fall issue of 1988, *The Piano Quarterly* published a list of the most frequently performed pieces from a sampling of 281 recitals. It will come as no surprise that Chopin won the sweepstakes prize hands down, emerging as the composer of almost one-fifth of everything played and certainly confirming Itzhak Perlman's lament that violinists lacked their Chopin.

Beethoven and Liszt were responsible for about 10 percent each, with Schumann, Schubert, and Brahms finishing in the money but trailing with single-digit-percentage status. Chopin's Nocturnes, Ballades, and Etudes finished win, place, and show, with his Scherzi only being nosed out by Debussy's Preludes, always a rambunctious filly. While not many surprises abounded, it was more comforting than otherwise to see Schubert's Impromptus, Haydn's Sonata in C (No. 50), and Scarlatti's Sonatas in the top twenty. Just below that group was Bach's highest finisher, the lovely Partitas.

The complete list may still be available by sending a stamped, self-addressed envelope to Joan Trapp, St. Ambrose University, 518 West Locust Street, Davenport, IA, 52803.

Oh, one bit of bad news. As pieces are learned to that point of proficiency where they approach being part of your desired permanent repertoire, they pass over into the maintenance mode, thus making room for others you are working on. The only trouble is that it is now necessary to increase the time devoted to practice since the newly admitted novices need to be played at least twice a week to keep them fresh.

Yeah, well. Often it is obligatory to let some material slip into desuetude. This is just another form of letting go. After all, you can't keep up everything you play. So when less demanding or less desirable pieces are demoted, just cast some of them off cheerfully in the knowledge that if you learned them once you can learn them again. Easy. Just accept it.

Chapter 9

Listening

Listening to piano music can bring a double pleasure to the dedicated amateur. There is, of course, the delight in the music itself but, additionally, there are the illumination and enhancement it can bring to one's own playing. That is, one can learn by absorbing everything one hears in a vast self-improvement vault. Timothy Gallwey stated it this way in his book, *Inner Tennis,* "one of the most important attributes of a good tennis player is that he possesses a memory bank filled with stored impressions of tennis experience — of balls going back and forth, body movements, forehands. . . . Tennis is learned as the nervous system coordinates the visual im-ages . . . with the feelings of the body's responses." Substitute notes for balls and aural for visual and you have it.

By way of example, at one time I was trying to improve my understanding of Liszt's "Mephisto Waltz." About two-thirds of the way through at the 3/8 time signature marked *con fuoco,* grandiose octave chords are struck with the right hand while a rich, thunderous waltz rhythm drives the left. The dense printing of notes on the page is daunting in and of itself. The complexity of notes and the total finger commitment had me so occupied that I was unable to focus on the sense of the composition at that point.

My frustration with the piece occurred just before a trip to Italy. Once there, I made a brief stop in a tiny out-of-the-way town near Parma called Sabbioneta, which at one time was referred to as the "Athens of Italy." It had been the pride and joy of an errant but knowledgeable member of the powerful Gonzaga family, who had left the intrigues and constraints of Milan to establish this minor Renaissance principality. Its main attraction was the Olympic Theatre, the first covered theatre in Europe, and one designed by Scamozzi. Mind you, this was a town of less than 5,000 people. Its roads were of simple, pounded dirt and stone and, except for the rare straggler such as myself, seldom played host to a tourist.

However, as I stood in front of the primitive building that housed the theatre I heard issuing forth from a window high above the street the very section of the "Mephisto Waltz" over which I had been laboring. Someone was playing it at about half speed on a slightly out-of-tune piano. Yet I was struck by a single arresting quality in the playing. Some special feature was causing the performance to be absolutely convincing, despite many repeats and a wrong note here and there.

It took a very short time to determine that the secret ingredient I was hearing even at that very slow tempo was a fervid commitment to a rock-solid rhythm. Even when the player repeated passages, he maintained a resolute beat tempered only so slightly by phrasing and dynamics. The beat was as convincing as a piledriver. Those great pickup notes on the second and third beats fell with such an insistent impact that the waltz tempo that followed never faltered. The pianist repeated parts over and over and never once broke stride.

I was in a daze of discovery. How could this challenging passage resolve itself into sanity and reason by simply slowing down and adhering to strict rhythm? The emphasis was so slight that I could hardly claim that it was a discovery, yet that undeniable pulse drove home the sense of the composition. *Rhythm above all else* I kept reminding myself. Now when I play that piece and come to that part I never fail to recall that crumbling, ancient street and those gorgeous, slow, persuasive sounds raining down on me from above and pointing the way.

Some teachers prefer that their students do not rely on recordings and live performances of others as their models for pieces they are studying. They argue that comprehension, style, phrasing, and all the rest should be acquired independently with no reliance on outside stimuli. They have a point when it comes to the tempos of the professionals, since quite obviously even your garden variety of concert pianist can generally outpace an amateur when it comes to finger dexterity and showmanship. Setting aside aberrations here and there, the public performer is generally going to play a vivace like a vivace, whereas in the hands of our standard-issue amateur it is more apt to emerge as an allegro, if not an allegretto.

The point here is that we often need to experience as many possible forms of stimulation to discover, undertake, and enhance our musical efforts. There is little question that our ears and the eyes are going to help us the most in this regard. Thus, every time we hear good musical examples, an intricate computer-like pattern takes shape in our nervous system whereby we tend to categorize the sounds we hear and form them into a complex structural framework that becomes our own personal text.

My example of the "Mephisto Waltz" was concerned with music heard live and directly. That is surely the purest and best form of perception and only one shade off of sitting face to face with the player in front of you or in the same room. However, running a close second to this sort of experience is music heard over radio or when watching television or a film. Since piano music, in particular, is a powerful, dramatic catalyst in creating mood, these media present constant sources of aural stimulation.

To name a few examples, Schubert is a trustworthy favorite for establishing an early nineteenth-century feeling. His work was used in both "Fanny and Alexander" and "My Brilliant Career," as well as in the sequel to the latter; Opus 90, No. 3, and parts of Opus 142 found good service throughout. Selections from Chopin Nocturnes, Mazurkas, Preludes, and Etudes pop up all the time, especially Chopin's A Major Prelude, F-sharp Nocturne, and the E Major Etude. In another recent television film the pianist brought the A-flat "Harp" Etude to a white-knuckle climax and was murdered right there on the bench for his efforts. The list is endless.

From time to time we benefit by being able to hear and see someone play a piece just a few feet away from us. Sometimes the music delivered at such close quarters by a gifted performer shows us a way to approach difficult material. Two examples come to mind.

Scriabin's Etude No. 12 in D-sharp minor has become a virtual Horowitz trademark. Lincoln Majorga has also played this dramatic piece several times on public television. Chiefly because of the demands for extended reaches in the left hand plus pulsating block chords in the right, the number is all but impossible for the amateur to play smoothly under any circumstances.

Consider my pleasure at hearing this piece played in a music store when I was buying some sheet music one day. The performer was a young, bearded man in jeans and polo shirt who started very softly and at a conservative tempo. He laid a foundation of granite, met the challenge of the formidable left-hand part, and wound up building strength and confidence as he worked his way to a magnificent climax and terminated things with a flourish. So much so that the few of us who were in the store gave him a cheerful round of applause.

Emboldened by that impromptu performance, I took another look at the awesome left hand and decided to elevate the work to the status of the Chopin Etude in Thirds, which is to say: a firm candidate for routine slow practice, preferably daily. Later I heard it used in the film *Madame Souzatska,* and noted that the playing of Yonty Solomon elevated it to a further high-water mark of taste. He seemed to make it flow in a linear fashion, whereas it had previously seemed more vertical—all starts and stops. It was a miraculous effect.

I had been slow to appreciate the pleasure which impressionist music could afford. Somehow its vaporous, seamless, slightly suspended quality put me off. However, one rainy day in San Francisco several years ago I was entering the main showroom of Sherman Clay on my way to the basement to buy some sheet music. Two men were standing by the imposing Bösendorfer 9′6″ Imperial taking off their raincoats. One of them began quietly working his way into Debussy's Prelude "The Sunken Cathedral." In a brief time he was filling the room with organ-like sound as he made his way to the mighty climaxes. I had stopped and stood transfixed at that ravishing sound. I assumed the performer was Garrick Ohlsson, a Bösendorfer artist at the time. The *San Francisco Chronicle* had announced that he was giving a concert that evening. His conviction and authority opened my eyes to the power and majesty of Debussy's art. There was nothing ephemeral or seamless about his treatment. It had rock-solid rhythm, melody, and form. It was a powerful performance of a powerful work.

Television can offer a rich feast for the amateur. I suppose the pinnacles would be the televised major competitions such as the Van Cliburn in Texas and the Tchaikovsky in Moscow. They leave one in awe of the marvelous gymnastics exhibited by the contestants. Such pyrotechnics aside, it is still possible to derive nourishment from presentations of individual pieces. Where you can obtain inspiration from the playing is often from the manner and style of the performer. Forgetting the matter of speed, there are often elements of hand and arm position, a picture of phrasing involving the body, and somewhat of an overview in approaching the material that can set an amateur off on a corrected course that he would never be able to perceive on his own.

During the last Tchaikovsky competition an unknown Russian youth was introduced who played the final movement of Beethoven's "Appassionata." He was too young for the competition at that time but was thought by virtue of his special gifts to be worth inclusion as a special feature of the program. He played like a young god in a somnambulant trance. His demeanor conveyed the impression that he owned the movement and had locked it up and thrown away the key. Wild cheers and bravos followed. Kisses were pressed on him by family and friends as he retreated into the wings. Two years later this pianist, Aleksei Sultanov, won the Van Cliburn International Piano Competition when "he rode the finale [of the "Appassionata"] to a glory to which many aspire but few achieve." If we were seeking inspiration there could be none greater.

Jorge Bolet presents a more austere, authoritative, if not severe, figure with which to deal. The good news for amateurs is that he has created several television Master Class programs of considerable quality. They are organized around some of his stellar students at the Curtis Institute where he heads the piano department. He comes on as a domineering ringmaster. Seated at the twin Bechsteins alongside his pupil, he wrings interpretive sense out of complex concerto and solo passages while his charges alternately sweat and flourish.

Bolet's memory and command of the material at hand are awesome. Like many stern performers whose power and wisdom are capable of assimilating the entire theatrical environment and bringing pressure to the boil, Bolet cracks the whip unremittingly. Then when the pressure would appear to be almost unbearable he extends a reassuring hand to the shoulder with a look of "job well done" that can produce an unexpected choke of emotion. He *is* a master, and these classes are worth searching for if they rerun on PBS or become available on videotape.

In Professor Edward W. Said's revelatory article in *Harper's* magazine about memorable performances, he wrote of virtuosity of style as well as simple pianistic excellence. The artists who impressed him most were Michelangeli, Richter, Gilels, De Larrocha, Pollini, Gould, Brendel, Kempf, Argerich, Lupu, and Perahia, to name a few. He emphasized their ability to tap into the subjective element in the listener, to "let the audience in," rather than repeat the same thing that has gone before. Their handling of secondary lines or themes is a very significant tool in their array of musical communications.

Listening Habits

There are a few basic procedures worth following that could make both casual and purposeful listening more worthwhile. The first is always to have a notebook and pen or pencil handy when you are apt to hear some music you might want to know about. The fact is that this could be almost *always,* so never be without something to write on. Get used to jotting down the *solfeggio* equivalents of the melody you hear. This is faster than trying to draw a staff and write out actual music. If we heard Chopin's A Major Prelude for the first time and wanted to identify it later, we would merely write: sol/mi, fa, re, re/re. la/fa#, sol, do, do/do., etc., or even abbreviating to s/m/f/r/r/r and l/f#/s/d/d/d.

There is no need to write treble clef or a key signature, and of course a flat can be noted with no difficulty when you are writing longhand. Then you have an adequate reminder of what you have heard. If the rhythm is tricky, you might want to embellish the slants indicating bar lines with some eighths, sixteenth notes, dots, and rests. However, it is really more useful to capture most of the melody than try to perfect the little bit you have.

Another great training tool is to listen to your records or CDs with the music itself in hand. All sorts of ideas come along that you will otherwise forget unless you make notes of them. Elsewhere we have discussed various ways of marking music to draw your attention quickly to the key parts of an enlightened performance. One of the chief elements that will pop out of artists' treatments of works you are studying will be the identification of those inner voices already discussed. These sometimes foster some artistic choices you never dreamed existed. Keep your penciled arrow working overtime as you aggressively highlight these artistic nuances. You will likely be able to incorporate some of them.

David Dubal's book of interviews, *Reflections from the Keyboard,* concludes with a rather complete discography of pianists' performances, which in many cases, as he points out, are the artists' own choices. Because of the rapid changes that are occurring in recorded music catalogues, my own choice here will be to conclude with a list of artists and selections that is geared to the current trend away from vinyl disc and cassette products with increasing emphasis on compact discs. In fact most of the discography choices are currently available on CDs.

The compact disc has come on the market under infinitely better auspices than was the case with cassette tapes or even vinyl recordings. In the case of recordings on vinyl there had initially been some confusion with regard to speed. This was quickly resolved, but for awhile some turntables were able to reproduce 78, 33, 45, and 16 RPM, the latter being the speed of some spoken records on the market. Cassettes, however, had the worst struggle. Not only was there a quality stigma due to the narrowness, slow speed, and high noise factor of the tapes, but there remains a lack of unanimity in worldwide marketing that has seen at various times reel-to-reel formats, eight-track, large cassette, mini-cassette, etc.

The chief accomplishment of the recording industry when contemplating the emergence of the compact disc was to work out international agreements and standards that, though they involved compromises, did permit the manufacture of machines and discs without fear by the makers or users that the format would undergo radical change in the short term.

With some compact disc players costing about the same as a decent turntable and cartridge, they represent a fine addition to home listening pleasure. But for compactness, longevity, and attractiveness of format, they are a particular boon to amateur pianists in assembling a true reference library of sounds. For these reasons they present advantages greater than those to other listeners.

For one thing, the harsh sound for which the compact disc can sometimes be criticized is least noticeable in its reproduction of piano music. For another, the format of the disc makes them ideal library tools for the student, since each selection is number coded and timed out in seconds with digital indices usually in an accompanying pamphlet.

The listener has only to punch up the track under study, repeat it if desired, and skip to whatever track is the next object of study. All this can take place with the remote control while seated at the keyboard. Fantastic. The advantage of the discs surviving careless treatment, scratches, bumps, and dings is obvious.

By good fortune and in anticipation of the coming CD market, companies began mastering digitally many years ago. Superb performances of almost all major works are in the archives of the major recording companies, many of them already having been released on vinyl recordings and a fair number on CDs.

Moreover, even valuable old master tapes and discs have been remastered with technology now available that renders them much more listenable than they were in the first place but also stabilizes them in an archival form on the compact disc that places them in a position of constant readiness for our future study. These recordings of legendary artists like Lipati, Cortot, Rosenthal, Lhevinne, early Horowitz, and Rubenstein and so many others are a part of our new-found legacy.

Each monthly issue of the *Schwann Catalogue of Records and Tapes* boasts numerous new CD offerings. It should now be possible to assemble a fairly complete library of fine piano recordings, utilizing, if we choose, compact discs exclusively. If our cup were not already overflowing we now have the science of Digital Audio Tape (DAT) on the horizon which promises all that the compact disc possesses, but more and better.

There is an unusual teaching tool available on recordings called *Music Minus One*. As the title of the series suggests, these are well-known works such as concertos, works for multiple pianos, also instrumentals, trios, quartets, and quintets, etc., that are designed with the elimination of a single instrument in the ultimate recorded performance so that the soloist can provide the missing part in his own surroundings. The piano music is included and is ingeniously cued to enable the pianist to find the tempo without benefit of a conductor.

The producers of this series have been criticized for maintaining tempi that, though perhaps correct, are too fast for the average or even better than average amateur. Their response has been that it would be a disservice to the composer and his work to perform it at a substandard tempo. The rebuttal to this expected defense might be that even among good conductors there is usually a fair latitude in rates of speed given one as against another. It would thus appear to have been the greatest service to those amateurs buying and attempting to play the records to favor the slower interpretations of the works over the medium or faster tempos. Such a policy would surely have done no violence to the composition as long as the tempo was within accepted boundaries. This seems not to have been the case. Even so, the records can be a great aid and should not be overlooked.

Now comes video tape piano instruction that must only be the tip of what will be a giant iceberg. *The Piano Quarterly* reviewed some of these in their Fall 1989 issue and will clearly be doing more of this in the future. Over half the titles reviewed seemed aimed at beginning students. Most advanced of the group presented featured the fine pianist and teacher Dorothy Taubman.

Having struggled with Liszt's "Variations on a Theme by Paganini" on my own, I was very impressed as I watched and heard the articulate Taubman leading her student through this intricate composition on video tape. Similar master classes with this superb instruction are available for Chopin's Scherzo in C-sharp minor and Beethoven's "Appassionata." Taubman is a scintillating mentor. A counter displays the seconds of running time so that the student can easily find parts of the tape he wishes to review. The production is exemplary. Send for information and brochure by addressing Enid Stettner, Executive Director, Dorothy Taubman Institute, Medusa, NY 12120.

Also available is an hour-long tape by Seymour Bernstein that complements his book, *With Your Own Two Hands.* I noted with specific interest his instruction on breathing, tips to relieve tension, and bench height. This material is available through Hal Leonard, Box 13819, Milwaukee, WI 53213.

Identifying Themes

This process of dredging up the names of specific movements from pieces is greatly aided by a theme index. One good example in print is Barlow and Morgenstern's *Dictionary of Musical Themes*, published by Crown. It is, of course, necessary to solidify the first six notes or so in your mind, whether by ironclad memory, jotting down of the notes or their solfeggio equivalents (do-re-mi, etc.), VCR, or cassette. This should be done accurately because it is amazing when trying to recall simple themes how deceptive the repetition of a note can be, not to mention the significance of an appoggiatura or a grace note.

I was watching a tape of *American Playhouse* on PBS and needed my memory jogged as to the lovely piano theme used at the beginning and end. For the purpose of using the theme dictionaries you first want to express the melody in the key of C or C minor like this:

G G G Ab Bb Ab Ab   S318

This series of notes appeared in the note index as G, G, G, A-flat, B-flat, A-flat, A-flat, G. Beside this combination is the code, S 361. Leafing back to the body of the book's hundreds of musical themes, you will quickly find this code in the Schubert section which is generally where I supposed it to lie but couldn't put my finger precisely on it. Sure enough, that was the second theme of "Moments Musicaux," No. 2.

Chapter 10

Environment, Health, and Ritual

Blaise Pascal, the seventeenth-century French philosopher, had much to say about man's resourcefulness, in addition, that is, to the wry advice about keeping out of mischief by sitting by himself in a room. Being alone, of course, does not exclude the presence of a piano. To that happy possibility we might add his further idea that an added cause of man's plight was his tendency to reminisce about the past, yearn for happiness in the future, and fail to cherish the present, which is, according to Pascal, all that is actually his.

He wrote,

> We are never content with the present moment. We anticipate the future . . . we call back the past . . . and neglect the only time that is ours. . . . The fact is that the present, as a rule, causes us pain. We hide it from sight, because it vexes us . . . and think to order things which are not within our control, against an hour which we have no certainty of ever reaching. . . . The present is never our end. Thus we never live, but only *hope* to live; and ever scheming to be happy, it is inevitable that we never are so.

It is on this precise point that we as lovers of the piano, insofar as we are and remain amateurs at least, are neither anticipating the future nor calling up the past. We are totally exploiting the present, in the best sense of that verb, perhaps borrowing some shading from the past for enhancement, but not unreasonably. Moreover, for most of the time we are, in fact, "alone in a room" as we study and practice, and presumably thus keeping those troubles at bay and our objectives elevated. No wonder you occasionally hear someone say, in referring to a rather insignificant amateur performance, "I'd give anything if I could play the piano like that." Such a fervent wish has less to do with envy of the pianist's physical dexterity than it does with what Pascal is talking about: a consciousness of the present as we players rejoice in the engagement of our playing, are enraptured by it, and are able to transmit our excitement. As a person who began the serious study of piano in his forties, I am obliged to argue that the thrill of the piano originates in the practicing. The sounds produced and altered, the goals achieved are as important to me as the satisfaction of playing a completed piece. The ideas merge.

On the other hand, I would have been no welcome newcomer next door to Thomas Carlyle's wife, Jane, who wrote, "Some new neighbors that came a month or two ago, brought with them an accumulation of all the things to be guarded against in a London neighborhood, viz., a pianoforte, a lap-dog, and a parrot," which assuredly shows us where we stand. This would tend to underscore the benefit to be had from playing where you disturb no one.

How is a potential battleground converted into a halcyon glade of concord? An acquaintance in a lovely Paris apartment on the Seine had solved the problem nicely. This happened to be an Italian lady on Quai Voltaire. Having recently bought the apartment and furnished its spacious living room with a concert Steinway and a Bösendorfer she went to her only immediate neighbors who could have been affected — those immediately above — and explained that she never got up until eight or nine o'clock and asked them what would be an agreeable termination hour, a time after which the piano would *never* be played unless special permission was requested. They said that ten o'clock at night would be fine. The result was that even though the boundaries were relatively rigid, my friend now had carte blanche for twelve hours, and achieved it with the neighbors in total accord. She could do whatever she liked with the piano inasmuch as a deal had been struck. On the other hand, if she had started things off by explaining that she liked to practice a lot and wondered when she might get in two or three hours of practice during the day and evening, the results could have been much more restrictive.

Acoustics, as we have discussed before, are a vital part of close-quartered living. If we are to be considerate of our neighbors, first we must demonstrate a sensitivity for the hours and volume of play. Second, we must divert some of our diligence toward our own comfort and the sounds that directly affect the player.

In addition to the hours of actual playing, there is the matter of loudness. Gordon Getty, the wealthy San Francisco composer, works on his compositions in a "studio soundproofed" room. Normally that description would imply that walls, ceiling, and floor "floated," and that the studio was virtually suspended in total insulation attained by containing its entire space and walls inside another outer space. Though not as costly as it sounds, this usually boils down to attaching surface finishing material like plaster, paneling, flooring, and ceiling panels to structural elements that are not *shared* by the finish materials of the opposite side. In other words, inside and outside finish surfaces have their own integrity and are not fastened to a common material such as the same studs or joists.

Acoustics play a major role in one's own enjoyment of playing the piano. So few people pay attention or do anything about subduing the reverberations within a room. The most forgiving surroundings are wall-to-wall carpeting set over concrete slab flooring. They are able to absorb the sound of almost any piano but the largest concert sizes (7'6" and 9'). Even the emanations of these large pianos might be contained if the ceilings were very high or irregularly pitched and the walls hung with thick fabric layers or special acoustic panels designed for this purpose. The point is that the room is there and the piano is there. It is up to you to manage the sound you produce so as to achieve the most pleasing effect on your ears.

In contrast to a slab, a hardwood floor can pose a menacing acoustic condition. It is made worse if there is a room below rather than natural soil, and worse yet if it is furnished with sparse area rugs, and a flat, smooth plaster ceiling, all of which pose the worst situation imaginable. With any luck of the draw your piano's habitat will fall somewhere in the middle of these extreme cases.

I have constantly had to fight off the problem of excessive reverberation in my own living room. It fairly fits the worst pattern of hostile ingredients imaginable, for although it contains the normal amount of rugs and upholstered furniture, there are hardwood floors, a full room below, nine-feet flat ceilings, with walls of paneling, plaster, or glass on all surfaces and only a scrap of drapery. So I took stock of the instruments. One was an old Hamburg Steinway concert "C" (7'5"), and the other, a Bösendorfer "200" (6' 7"). They each gave off distinctly different sounds. When I listened to another person play either one of them it would produce gorgeous but uniquely divergent tones. These pianos were each happy and beautiful sounding in their own way (when heard from a distance), but acoustically annoying when I played them over a long period of time. Then they were both unhappily different.

The Steinway sounded aggressively frontal from the moment a note was struck. It vibrated right down to the floor. It gave off a facile, big, full, brilliant tone that was hard to control. What it did best was perform a booming double-forte with concert hall splendor. Middle to lower bass notes growled and merged, with pianissimo subtleties being beyond it. It gobbled up pieces in the heavy romantic idiom and yearned to emit its lush, deeply colored sounds, those that suited the more orchestral writing of later Beethoven, Chopin, Liszt, Brahms, and Schumann, and, of course, Rachmaninoff. If I played it for an extended period of time I would become fatigued.

In contrast, the Bösendorfer welcomed you to its cushioned keybed and invited you to go to the bottoms of the notes without threatening that it would bite you back. Oftentimes its silvery daintiness tended to set up an almost electronic image in the frequencies below middle C. This effect no doubt had much to do with my own over-resonant acoustics. Yet it excelled at baroque and classic music up through early Beethoven and picked up again with the impressionist works of Debussy and Ravel. It also played great jazz and left little doubt as to why Oscar Peterson has become one of Bösendorfer's enthusiastic concert artists.

Both pianos in differing areas of performance shared the fault of overwhelming the player with excessive sound. I did several things to try to rectify this. The first was to increase rug coverage underneath and around the pianos by supplementing the throw rugs and strewing about a variety of cushions which I tipped up against the legs and pedal lyres.

I tried inserting padding material directly under the sound board using one-inch, medium-density foam. The trouble with this method was that the sound waves penetrated the padding or foam and continued on their downward path to the floor and around the room, bouncing as they went. The essential thing seemed either to redirect them or to trap them. I subsequently gave up on this method after concluding that it altered the tone without greatly reducing volume.

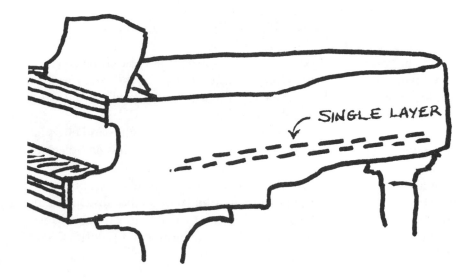

I then tried adding another layer of foam directly under the first. I suspended a three-inch-thick piece of dimpled foam a few inches below to attempt to trap the sound.

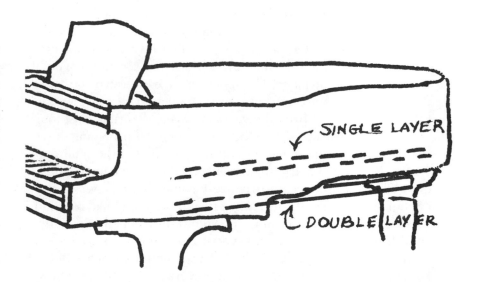

This unattractive arrangement did mute the downward thrust of sound somewhat but still left the player at the mercy of all the volume coming from the top of the piano.

The room remained so alive with sound that I asked an acoustics engineer to analyze the sound characteristics of the room and to "mike" it or meter it—as their terminology goes—and tell me what could be done to reduce the reverberation.

This scientist strode into the room, looked around and clapped his hands together smartly a few times. Upon hearing no echo, he said, "I have all the instruments in the car to create a report of detailed sound measurements, but I can tell you merely from the deadness of my hand claps that there is plenty of sound absorption in here. You had better focus on the placement of your pianos. Move them out from the corners and add a few more sound blotters. The room itself is fine."

His simple hand claps had demonstrated that there was no undue resonance from the space itself. He had to be right. I should have known enough to have checked that myself, but it was so simple that it had never occurred to me. So I pulled them out into the room a couple of feet and also placed the pianos on large insulated caster bases. These caster bases were laminated with one or two circular patches of dense rubber glued to the bottom. They seemed to reduce floor reverberation somewhat and helped diffuse and isolate the sound. The type of caster base available in hardware stores is only useful for ordinary domestic furniture and will not accept the weight or caster size of a grand piano. The special wide bases can be obtained from a piano supply store or from your technician. The fact remained that the extra distance from the corners plus added rugs, cushions, and caster bases solved part of the environmental problems.

However, two additional procedures completed the taming of my beasts. Primarily I began to concentrate on my own image of the tone I wished to produce and realized, somewhat to my surprise, that I could manipulate the ultimate effect more than I had realized. The second part of transforming my sound into something angelic resulted from several meaningful voicing sessions with my technician. He identified notes that I liked already on the pianos, listened to them in various parts of the room, and worked slavishly to achieve a uniform, full, rounded sound. It was a miracle. Everything came together. No more thick pads and rugs and tricky acoustic shields were necessary. I had found a balance.

Apart from not crowding the corners or walls, the single most effective weapon in combating excessive sound due to the room or instrument or both was a modification of my own performance and touch. I even found that it was easier and more relaxing to practice when I focused on producing the most beautiful tone possible. If you have a really bad situation, such as an apartment where *no* piano playing is acceptable, you can consider getting a clavichord or electronic keyboard and headset.

When not in use, a fine, well-tuned, well-voiced piano should be kept closed. There are 12,000 parts in a grand piano, which is to say that it is infinitely more complicated than a violin or a cello, both of which usually remain in their cases when they are not being played. Furthermore, if your piano is in the path of a constantly open window or doorway, it should also be at least partially covered *even when closed* to keep moisture and dirt from having their way since rust is the worst enemy of all.

Clothing may seem like a frivolous subject to introduce when discussing art. In cool weather it seems almost unnecessaary to recommend wearing loose, comfortable clothing in which to practice. However, I think of Ned Rorem and Vladimir Ashkenazy in their throttling turtleneck sweaters and I do so. These may be alright in an icy auditorium but not in the average home where a quirk of mine is to try to maintain the room a few degrees cooler than what could be called "shirt sleeve" temperature, that is something for idle lounging. About 66 degrees happens to work for me, but we all have slightly different body thermostats.

You maintain your own warmth by wearing a light sweater or jacket. That is much better than relying on an entire room of air so warm that you could comfortably prance around naked. Such an environment tends to make one wilt after a while and thwarts concentration. Short of sitting with teeth clenched and skin turning blue, tempt the elements by allowing a wee portion of cold to get to your body. The theory is that you will not get chilled through that way. Recall that our primary objective throughout practice is to heighten consciousness, to which end you can enlist your environment as an ally — stopping just short of a woolly turtleneck.

Considering all that has been written about health, diet, exercise, vitamins, etc., it is unlikely that we can add much to those areas that has not already been stated. However, there is one fact that the most redoubtable skeptic might have to admit as being true with regard to the piano. Unassailable is the fact that it is extremely hard to play the piano well for a long period of time if you feel lousy. By which I mean that if you are tired, worried, nervous, preoccupied, not to mention hung over, ill with a cold, hay fever, runny nose, asthma, headaches, fever and so on, you will have an uphill struggle on your hands and are probably wasting your time. This commitment to mental concentration, physical coordination, stamina, and willpower is simply too complex and demanding for serious practicing if you are in less than top physical condition.

Early Morning

My own routine, since I start quite early with practice and devote two hours to it, is to let the piano flower, so to speak, as my own sequence of keyboard tasks unfolds. I begin with the piano lid down, generally laying a foundation of Bach. Then I work on things in rotation as under Repertoire. I progress into some separate projects or on to the Chopin Etudes followed by some Preludes. About then I take a break. When I resume practicing I usually raise the piano lid and become more expansive. I look forward to the change in tonal quality and volume and respond to the extra excitement of music-making.

Books on occupational health devote chapters to advising transcontinental truck drivers, draftsmen, business men, and other lengthy chair-sitters how to deal with their occupational petrification. Since exercise will not combine easily with these sedentary pursuits it is essential periodically to interrupt one's static pose at the keyboard and adopt, if you will, an opposing stance of some kind. In the case of pianists, a knee-to-chest position as in the example of a trucker hiked up in his cab berth, allows the organs and muscles, veins and arteries to experience some relief from the punishing rigidity of extended sitting and concentration. A short period of upending oneself in this topsy-turvy position creates a sort of beneficial reverse polarity. Surely every twenty or thirty minues you deserve some sort of break, and if you cannot walk or run around conveniently these upside-down stretching and displacement techniques employed for three or four minutes should do the trick in reestablishing your vitality.

Who is not short of time? Now with the addition of practice time, the shortage can become even more severe. Arnold Bennett cautioned to shun the tyranny of morning newspapers. That is a start. If he had known about the U.S. shower syndrome he would doubtless have fought off that as well in order to clean the early morning decks for meaningful action. The point here is to get to work and practice first thing. It is the most valuable time you have.

Nourishment

In getting a flying start on the practicing, put aside any thoughts of food. Limit yourself to a cup of coffee for about three-quarters of an hour. That is a perfect length of time to accomplish a minimum session at the keyboard.

In Dubal's *Reflections from the Keyboard*, Tomás Vásáry attributes the conquering of a rusty muscular feeling and excessive pain in the joints to a meatless diet. Forced to give up meat for a different reason, he noticed that his pain and discomfort had subsided, so he decided to eliminate meat as a permanent regime. "All my life," he said, "I had been a heavy meat eater; and ever since I stopped eating it, my hands have felt better."

Once in a restaurant in Venice I heard a naïve, young American couple ask the waiter if the beef consommé had any meat in it. He held up his open palms to them and looked at the ceiling. "Oh, no, no. No meat at all. No meat at all," he said, as if horrified at the thought. He brought the soup, and they slurped it down in contented bliss, never inquiring about the origin of the soup stock.

Theories abound on what dietary disciplines might alleviate pain from joint swelling or inflammation. It is hard to believe, given what even laymen know about diets and nutrition these days, that heavy meat consumption can benefit these conditions. Excessive acid—wine, citrus, coffee, vinegar, etc.—might also be looked at as detrimental to good health. Beyond that it would appear to be a matter, as in so many other areas of physical well-being, of genes, regular exercises, a positive attitude, and a great deal of luck.

Evening Practice

Pick up what additional practice time you can in the evening. I don't happen to like to practice after eating. I just feel a little less sharp after a nice luncheon or, particularly, after dinner. Actually the time *before* dinner I have found to be an excellent period for a concentrated hour of practice, as I assume Thomas Jefferson did when he recommended that his eleven-year-old niece practice one hour a day before her dinner. That combined commitment should assure meaningful progress as time goes on.

Although mentioned previously under separate categories, the subject of assigning exercises to students comes up again under this heading of health. Dorothy Taubman, renowned teacher and expert on musicians' injuries, notes in *The Piano Quarterly*, "I never assign exercises. I disapprove of them because they are often responsible for injuries. Finger individualization exercises (pulling up each finger separately away from the other fingers) are cripplers. You can't stretch the small muscles of the fingers without eventually causing damage...students do the exercises with the same inordinate movements that caused the passage to fail in the first place."

A recent Purdue University study of concert performers showed that playing with straight fingers was more apt to cause injuries than the traditional curved hand method. The researchers stumbled on this knowledge by calculating the forces at various crucial finger joints and tendons.

While not impugning the validity of this study nor the efficacy of the arched hand and finger position, I dissuade anyone committing to one hour or two of daily practice from starting all over again if his normal position is more or less flat. I believe more can be done through arm rotation and modification of pressure applied to keys to assuage the threat to life and limb.

As stated before and as supported by Ms. Taubman, most problems of so-called technique can be solved by forearm rotation. The keys to healthy playing are:

- Finger motion aimed at the *point of sound*;
- Finger destination that rests at the bottom of the key;
- Forearm rotation to assist in lateral movement;
- Fingering studied to avoid stretching and twisting.

The Piano Quarterly and *Keyboard Classics* have over the years both devoted considerable space to the problem of pianists' health.

A few truths surface: Do not overdo; stop and rest if something hurts; if you cannot concentrate easily, it is a signal to stop; if you feel tense, try to relax physically and mentally, and breathe deeply; and finally think of your whole body, not just your fingers.

Physical Exercise

There seems little doubt that even if exercise does nothing to prolong life, it certainly makes a lot of us feel better, improves muscle tone, helps keep weight off, and may, if done correctly and with sound objectives in mind, keep the circulatory and respiratory systems somewhat more resistant to failure. Although it will never succeed forevermore, the habit of frequent exercise does what can only be done for a while, to keep Mother Nature at bay.

Because of its sedentary nature, playing the piano for hours each day should be supplemented by some form of exercise. Whether it is running, biking, rowing, fencing or what have you, your command of the keyboard and ability to concentrate will be enhanced by exercise. At the very least the pianist's day should include thirty minutes of very purposeful walking of about two miles. Full, deep breathing while at the keyboard will promote relaxation. So too will a comfortable upright posture, straight back, and good light. With all of these physical elements in gear, your playing will thrive.

If you are an older amateur and particularly if you have started this lengthy practicing later in life, it is probable that you will some day experience some hand pains. You should mention this to your doctor during normal physical examinations. Quite a few doctors are knowledgeable in sports and music and are usually quite interested in patients' problems with these activities, many of which they share. Try to obtain your physician's latest thinking on whatever physical obstacles you have. Whatever you do, make your approach on the basis of your continuing commitment to playing, just as if you were a professional and expected to be treated like one. The danger in being advised to stop playing for any significant period is in thinking that you can start up again any time that you like. Don't count on it. The chances of getting going again after a lengthy layoff are slim indeed.

On the subject of exercise, young Feghali, who won the 1985

Van Cliburn competition in Texas, said that swimming was the best exercise for a pianist. Surely tennis would not be risky for the amateur, since any of the injuries incurred in that sport are usually to the legs and feet. Even the dreaded tennis elbow should not affect one's piano-playing muscles. However, serious walking remains the trustworthy standby that little else can equal.

Hardly an exercise, but not less dangerous is the seemingly comradely event of having your hand shaken. There are still manual squeezers out there who loom like bullies in a schoolyard. You should approach any of those fearful introductory rites with reasonable caution. A good ploy is to attempt to slide your hand well up toward the wrist of the opponent where the bases of the palms meet. This tends to thwart a vigorous gripper. The risk is that once ensheathed in such a grip you are so far committed to this hand embrace that if the adversary chooses to override your gambit with a desperate squeeze, perhaps employing reinforcement with his left hand, you are a goner.

Someone has said that most of the complex work of the world is done by people who do not feel well. It would be hard to believe that many sonatas and concertos are being played by people who are under the weather. Too much concentration, memory work, muscular coordination, and overall philosophical buoyancy is required to perform these complex works. Above all, feel good about yourself. Keep your mind and body healthy. Whatever else you do, *don't stop!*

Chapter 11

Practicing on the Move

A man's village is his peace of mind.

Anwar al-Sadat

The homely, self-contented spell of the fireside and coziness of imagined village life have enchanted me from my earliest years. I am possessed with a strong tendency to nest, whether I am at home or in some distant place. It makes little difference where I am, the urge is identical, either to transform it into a replica of home and all that it means or, failing that, to explore and compare the qualities that make it different, trying to redefine what life must be like there. The availability of a piano while traveling poses a major challenge to this attitude. It has led me into some interesting byways and acquaintances in the United States and abroad.

A usable piano, as you might guess, is not the easiest thing to find in a foreign country. In the course of a dozen trips to Europe, mostly concentrated in England, France, and Italy, I developed some unique and valued associations with people and pianos that sometimes led to enriching practice time and sometimes to disappointment and frustraton. Often ironic, these piano quests are offered as *petites amuse-gueules* for kindred souls who seek pianos to keep up their own practice. Let us hope you can derive some inspiration from this.

Dry Practice

The well-known pianist Ruth Slenczynska was a child prodigy and is presently a concert and recording artist who teaches at Illinois

State University. Through some correspondence she was the first to introduce me to the right kind of silent practice keyboard. No mere piece of folded cardboard, the drawing and instructions she sent me were for a truly simulated piano keyboard with all the "feel" that entails except, of course, the movement of the keys. I made one myself without much difficulty.

The materials required were:

- 2 pieces of ¾″ plywood smooth on one side (8″ × 30″);
- a complete set of plastic piano keys obtainable from any piano supply shop at reasonable cost or from your piano technician, since some stores will not sell to retail customers;
- glue-backed green protective felt from any hardware store, enough to pad the underside of the plywood;
- 2 brass hinges 2″ × 3″ and screws;
- a small bottle of contact cement.

The object is to glue down the keys just as they are positioned on a standard piano keyboard. You can mark these spaces out carefully with a pencil and start gluing the keys down. Allow for normal key spacing by using any appropriate spacers like small 6-penny finish nails, being sure to allow for the hinged crack between the two pieces of plywood which should occur between B-flat and B just below middle C.

Middle C

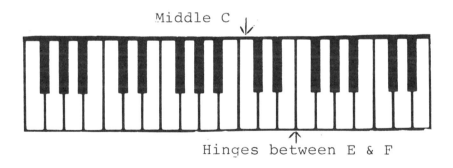

Hinges between E & F

As Madame Slenczynska advised me, this device enables one to keep up silently with the "geography" (her charming word) of the keyboard at all times with a minimum subtraction from normal luggage space. In addition to its use in travel, this same practice keyboard can serve you if you suffer the bad luck of having to spend any time in bed and feel like practicing. Anyway, it's a good little project however you approach it.

England

London, that most musical of cities, virtually pulsates with music colleges, church organs and choirs, large and small concert halls, publications about music, libraries, music stores, piano stores, and never ending concerts and recitals. It is the music capital of the world. For teachers, students, and amateurs it is a tonal mecca. It would not only be impossible to attend all of the concerts and recitals, but it would even be impossible to know about them.

As to practice facilities for the individual, they are easy to find. My own hotel offered me the use of two pianos. The hours were too restrictive on the nice grand in the lounge, and I was concerned about interfering with cleaning and setting of tables in the dining room during its off hours, where the other small vertical one was located. However, I did try the console once or twice just for the fun of it.

Various rental studios are listed in the yellow pages of the telephone book, but more satisfactory were the practice studios of the Bösendorfer London Piano Centre just above Oxford Street next to Wigmore Hall. Also the tiny St. Albans studio just south of Picadilly Circus offered three practice rooms and was usually easy to book. Some piano stores had rental studios, but the two mentioned above were the most convenient and accessible for me.

Rates were around three to five pounds an hour at both places. The Bösendorfer studios' twenty-five to thirty practice rooms were equipped with very tired old Kimball baby grands (the Kimball Company owns Bösendorfer) that had not only seen better days but were never going to see them again. They were getting ready to join S. Erard and J. Steinweg on the big soundboard in the sky.

Nevertheless, they could be adequate for practice so far from home. Most of the studios had large windows looking onto the street, so that on a damp, drippy, Jack-the-Ripper sort of rainy London night, the short breaks from playing could afford a fine, protected view of the slick street and threatening weather.

On my journeys to and from the practice rooms and restrooms I would hear a cacophonous symphony of scalings, crashing chords, arias, small string groups, brass ensembles, tinklings, trillings, and even a quartet of snare drums. More regal was the right to pass over the thick maroon carpet and among the highly polished beautiful new pianos on the first two wood-paneled sales floors. This magnificently appointed sanctum induced hushed voices, reverential stares of appreciation, and, occasionally, serious masterly playing. I obtained permission on more than one visit to try some notes on these gorgeous-sounding Bösendorfers before trudging up the stairs to my monk's cell.

By contrast, the St. Albans studios were in a crowded, ill-kept basement complex of three studios run by an engaging woman, Jessica Landor, and her bright family. They boasted a gentlemanly old Blüthner and serviceable Schnabel, both small grands. Arrangements here were less formal and more flexible. On a floor somewhere above was even an apartment available with its own piano. If this were not enough, the Italian restaurant on the ground floor was open most hours of the day and night and served up quite good espresso coffees and cappuccinos to go. Not bad.

London, because of its central layout and feet-kindly distances, turns out to be an ideal city in which to try all the major pianos at the various dealers. Almost all of them are within walking range. Every make is represented there and, of course, language is not a barrier. There are many shops selling sheet music, with two of the best being Foyles and Peters.

Normally unavailable to the amateur are the studios of the Society of Concert Pianists on Bedford Street, for perhaps reasons implicit in the name. Unless one has a special means of entrée, only qualified concert artists need apply there. Still, it is good to know that it exists. It should come as no surprise that the studios therein sport only Steinways and that the charge for use is many pounds an hour. Transportation of music while traveling can be a problem, particularly if you try to take too much. This is an area where one has to be ruthless. I bought a six-partition fiber expansion file at the stationery store before leaving, the kind that ties with a thin wraparound ribbon. Stuffing it to a thickness of about two and one-half inches I was able to take with me the core of my current projects plus some essential staples like the Chopin Etudes. However, the bulk of what I carried was made up of single editions, and I made it a point not to take one single scrap that was not going to be practiced often. A more sophisticated approach would be to carry music of reduced size which could be made up on any good copying equipment.

France

The biggest and most impressive group of studios in Paris are in the multi-storied Salles Pleyel near Place de l'Etoile. Many activities are housed under this one historic roof. The Symphony of Paris has its headquarters there. Complete floors are devoted to dance and voice. It exudes a large-scale, institutional feeling that reminds one of a vast inner-city professional school dedicated to the arts like the New York one in *Flash Dance,* but in more elegant housing with a full concert hall included.

It also remains institutional, that is to say bureaucratic, when it comes to trying to engage a studio. The first person with whom I talked said that there were no times available nor empty studios. A second person was more tractable and produced a contract for signature and request for full payment in advance. All dates and times were set in advance.

Some part of the utility company brusqueness is forgivable when you comprehend the size of the building and the large office staff needed to run it and the concert hall as well. In fact, during the various weekday mornings when I booked space there were scores of empty rooms. Maybe the apparent empty rooms could be accounted for by their having been contracted in large blocks over long periods, perhaps months. Who knows?

The pianos were mediocre little consoles but adequate for routine, maintenance practice. The studios at Salles Pleyel had windows that could be opened. When walking through the bulding and around the corridors you became aware of the intense vitality present in clusters on the various floors. In order to glimpse the interior of this beehive, I once stole to the end of a hallway that revealed a forbidden entrance to the concert hall. Through a small window I saw the Orchestra of Paris being led by a woman conductor in Debussy's "Afternoon of a Fawn." It was ravishing. This whole experience was worth the vexation of the initial negotiation.

Although it is not central to much of anything, the Daniel Magne Bösendorfer Piano Center on Rue Raymond-Poincare is located in the Seizième Arrondisement near Place Victor-Hugo. It is a first-class haven for amateurs. The most convenient Metro stop is the Trocadero, right near the Palais de Chaillot. This impressive showroom is positioned in one of the best residential areas of Paris, the Seizième being highly sought after because of its nearness to the

Bois de Boulogne, its relative quiet, and its reasonable distance from the heart of Paris.

Row upon row of fine apartment buildings line the wide street. Place Victor-Hugo and its spoke-like tributary streets form a neighborhood that is well worth exploring. For good measure there was a fine music shop lying just between the Bösendorfer studio and Place Victor-Hugo called Pierre Schneider, located at 61, Ave. Raymond-Poincaré.

All the rental instruments including the verticals were in nearly new condition at the Bösendorfer studios. The premises were attractive and clean, and the personnel very accommodating. Naturally the facilities were greatly in demand by amateurs, professionals, and teachers, so it was necessary to plan well ahead, preferably by writing or calling before even leaving home as I did. I found it necessary to allow plenty of time getting to and from the studio, since it was located in a high density area for people and cars.

One night at dinner a friend asked if I would like to see her cousin's apartment where she had two pianos. While they couldn't be played because of the late hour, I still wanted to absorb what it would be like to function as an amateur pianist in a truly Parisian domestic setting.

Our taxi let us off on the busy Quai Voltaire before a pair of very tall doors wedged between the commercial stores that line the land side of that thoroughfare. The pressing of a buzzer brought an immediate squawk from the tiny speaker and the buzz of a latch. We entered a large, dark courtyard and proceeded toward a flight of steps to the upper level where a door was standing open. I entered a huge, high-ceilinged living room, smelling of fresh paint and new carpeting. The lights of the Seine and those of the Louvre lay beyond. There was a gorgeous 9′ Hamburg Steinway concert grand and, as if that were not enough, a choice, smaller Bösendorfer.

I was thrilled when the cousin asked me to return the next day and play for as long as I wished during daylight hours. Late the next morning I dropped by and found the Steinway to be the usual big, full, rich performer I had supposed. The Bösendorfer produced a light, mellow, silvery tone. Alternating between the two, I would fall in love with one, then race to the other as if I were alternately tasting a glass of 1961 La Tache and another of 1958 Chateau Latour, each requiring a brief grace period of adjusting the senses, and sometimes the manner of play. Once done, each offered an abundance of astounding beauty. A year or so later I ran across a reference in *A Virgil Thomson Reader* to one of his periods of Paris residence when his apartment had been located at that exact address on Quai Voltaire.

Italy

Not without cause, Verona is called "the Little Florence." The Adige runs through it just as the Arno runs through Florence. There are cypress-covered hills to form a background, as there are the requisite quattrocento amenities consisting of a classic old-town center, two major piazzas, a ruined arena, an arch, a bridge, and an old castle. What it doesn't have is so many people. At about half the size of Florence, it has fewer residents and far fewer tourists. It is more manageable as a city to use and enjoy. Nowhere was this more evident than during the delightful hours of practice spent there.

The Hotel Due Torri, where I stayed, had a typical "buca" or cave as its underground cocktail lounge. A nighttime bar that is dormant the rest of the day can cause the nostrils of a pianist to flare. I had written to the manager before leaving home informing him of my intended stay and got a nice letter in return saying that he would welcome me and arrange some hours when I could practice. He was true to his word; he greeted me personally and on more than one occasion escorted me to the basement and admitted me to the locked room and helped turn on the lights to boot. That sanctum housed a well-tuned, lively Schimmel console that I remember for its dainty felt keyboard cover bearing the name of a Veronese piano dealer.

I would go down about eight in the morning and work for two hours. The rest of the day was free for sight-seeing on foot and meals with friends. The central area of Verona, the Piazza delle Erbe, was within walking distance.

On my last day after a pleasant luncheon at the venerable Tre Corona near the arena, I strolled down the broad Corso Porto Nuova through a newer area. With no trouble at all I found the piano store whose felt cover had lain over the hotel's little console. I offered to buy one but instead was given two as gifts.

The physical structure of Venice suggests that there would be a minimum of pianos available, perhaps establishing some sort of Guinness record for "city with the least pianos," perhaps positioning it in hot contention with perched villages and Alpine monasteries. The pianist's problems would be solved if he were to plan to stay at the Europa Hotel inasmuch as it has a piano bar like the Due Torri. Except there is one major difference. Venice's underground situation being what it is, bucas are out and what has to serve instead is a glassed-in bar off the main lobby. Even if you stayed there and arranged for some off hours with a friendly concierge, practicing in that setting would have been like playing in an emptied aquarium.

At the Gritti, Danielli, Cipriani, and Bauer Grunwald, any pianos are too exposed and not appropriate for our purpose here. There would be no way to feel comfortable practicing unless you wanted to submit to the useless exercise of playing some subdued nocturnes for a few minutes and scampering off when the curious gathered around.

A concierge at the Gritti told me that he could arrange for the use of a piano at La Fenice, the legendary Venice opera house. What could have been better? I reported there on instructions from the hotel several times. Each time I penetrated a little farther into the labyrinthine bowels of that jewel of a building. I finally made it all the way up to the director's office where I was told by the most compassionate but firmest of Englishmen — for that is what he turned out to be — that not only were the overcrowded rehearsal halls no place for an amateur to practice but that he had never heard of anyone from the Gritti contacting him in the first place. From the bedlam of tuning up, scales, do-re-mi-fa-sols, dancing and twirling in every nook and cranny, and smells of paint, powder, and floor wax, I felt that the rebuff was completely justified.

I told this little tale of woe to a gathering of concierges which had sympathetically accumulated behind the formidable desk in the lobby. There was ample manifestation of genuine grief over my predicament, no matter how it had occurred. Mouths scowled downward; eyes beseeched heavenward. One helpful soul — Mario? Carlo? which was it? — ventured the explanation that Communists intervened too much in personal matters that were best handled between individuals as they had in the old days. Who was I to gainsay?

Mario, on whom I had relied the most, clapped his palms together as if seized with a sudden urge to prey. Perhaps in an attempt to justify the tip he had already pocketed, he gently suggested I go on another quest he had devised.

"Signor," he said. "I know of a teacher of piano music who will surely let you use his piano. It only remains for you to negotiate with him."

I had nothing to lose. My days there were numbered anyway. He told me to go to a certain address past the Rialto Bridge near the Campo Beccarie where at a specified apartment a Signor Caesare St. Angelo would receive me and where I could no doubt practice on his piano. After all, he was involved in music for money, wasn't he? It sounded logical. So it was only proper that I cough up another 10,000 lire note.

At six o'clock, the appointed hour, on a dark and rainy night that would have done justice to *Death in Venice* or *Don't Look Now*, I penetrated well past the Rialto to the Beccarie. Intrepidly I groped my way to a dimly lit set of iron gates. I pressed the button of the number given and heard an electronic buzz. I entered a dank, untended garden. I heard the clearing of a throat and a gentle call from a lighted doorway a flight above. I ascended some mean steps to meet Signor St. Angelo.

At the entrance of the apartment stood a young, bearded man of about thirty clad in a V-necked sweater and dark velvet pants. He motioned me with signs elaborate enough to show that he either could not or would not be speaking any English. This would add an extra dimension to our negotiation.

I began by agonizing through my few rudimentary phrases of Italian, the sort of thing that gets you by in hotels and restaurants. Even this feeble exchange flashed a kleig light of truth on the fact that *he* expected to be the one interviewed with the prospect of my asking him to be my teacher. By some insane logic my mentor at the hotel had supposed that I could talk him into sitting idly and no doubt angrily by while I banged about on his keyboard just for the fun of it. Weird scene.

Caesare motioned me into the living room where there stood an attractive 7' Steinway grand and little else. He sat at the bench and rustled through a stack of music on the floor, threw something up on the music rack and began to play, assuming that I would remain standing at his side. For the better part of an hour I stood riveted there like a post without removing my raincoat. At appropriate intervals I turned pages for him, knowing now that I would never get to play.

He plowed through an amazing succession of ambitious music. The first was Chopin's "Polonaise Fantasie," throughout which he committed endless errors but in that weaselly way musicians sometimes do that conveys their knowledge of the piece but recent lack of practice. I continued turning. Next was the Ballade in F minor, Ballade in A-flat, the Barcarolle, and four movements, including the interminable third, of the Sonata in B minor. He concluded with four Debussy pieces, "Reflets dans l'Eau," "Hommage à Rammeau," "Mouvement," and "Poissons d'Or," all one after the other. It was a healthy dose of piano music.

Caesare was a pale, thin man of medium height with leprous white, elongated hands and long, untapered fingers with curiuosly spatulate tips, not bad tools for a pianist's work. I saw Oscar Peterson's hands in a close shot one time, and they looked quite similar. Almost as if to prove their aptness, in the final movement of the Chopin Sonata, he brandished his skinny hands to show that he could execute the tenths and elevenths of the left without the need of a full rotation, but more as if they were mere triads.

Finally he asked me to play something for him at long last, and in pent-up frustration I dove into the opening of the Brahms Paganini Variations which was much too difficult for me to attempt under pressure. Then, breaking off, I tore off on the Chopin Etude in C, Opus 10, No. 1, at much too fast a tempo and couldn't command my right hand to rotate in the approved manner. I flubbed it badly. Because I was sweating and producing too many wrong notes, I took off my raincoat, then tore off the jackets under that and dashing both to the floor, rolled up my sleeves, cleaned my glasses, drew a fresh breath, and was ready to play.

He said, "We must go now."

Moving toward the door I struggled to worm out some facts. I learned that he was languishing, being overworked and underpaid in a job as a high school teacher of music theory. He worked in the mainland industrial adjunct of Venice, Mestre. This slavery permitted him no time to practice. While he had escaped obligatory military service it had only been because of a deviated septum which not only caused him severe migraine headaches, the pain of which would have curtailed practice even if he had had the time, but necessitated an operation that he both feared and could not afford.

The truth is, I liked Caesare. Had I been staying on I would like to have taken some lessons from him, provided that I could have logged some practice time on his piano. The obstacle of the language barrier would have been surmountable after a while. Teaching, after all, was his profession. Moreover, there exists no greater teacher of languages than the need to get a job done. A crew of workers in a boat, a kitchen, a jail, a mine, a lighthouse, or an airplane will get to the heart of communication speedily. So in music, the very subject provides the structure for the needed intercourse, and one's desire for study and understanding becomes the impetus.

Caesare never tried to explain his use of the apartment. Had I become his pupil I surmised that we might have been able to use it for our lessons together. Practice on my own would have been left up to me. Many questions remained unanswered. Were we in the quarters of an eccentric uncle? A pixilated auntie? The greatest imponderable lingered until the last. I had been on my feet for well over an hour turning his pages and sweating in my raincoat. After leaving him I would face another long walk over the Accademia Bridge and on almost to the Zattere. Venice being what it is, with not a lot of friendly bars and hangouts on every corner, especially on a drippy, fog-shrouded night like that, as I started putting on my raincoat and leaving the doorway, I cast an eye about and asked, "Puedo usare il W.C.?"

"No," he said to my unbelieving ears. "Ha preso quest' appartimento a prestito." (I am only borrowing it.)

I send Caesare St. Angelo a Christmas card every year and wish him well. I hope he has scraped together enough courage and money to have his operation. It would stop the headaches and, provided he can get a better job, make it possible for him to practice as he should. He told me his favorite piano recordings, those by artists he most admires, are by Horowitz, Arrau, and De Laroccha. I think of him often and his beautiful, wasted talent and that luscious, flawed playing. There must be so many Caesares.

Two days before leaving Venice I was taken by a gondolier acquaintance to the apartment of his lady friend. Her pleasant quarters were near the railroad station and the old ghetto and housed a Steinway and Bechstein grand. She had been an American law student married to an Italian musician whose untimely death had left her as a permanent expatriate. She graciously let me play to my heart's content and even offered me a glass of wine when I was through. With only one day remaining she insisted that I come again. It was impossible. All I could do with time left that last day was to take her a small gift of appreciation. I left Venice consumed with profound regret that I had not met this wonderful lady earlier, but such is the luck of itinerant amateurs. Venice isn't easy.

The passion for keeping up with practice while traveling finds some people feeling guilty because such behavior is an unfit subtraction from sightseeing, shopping, and dining; those being the proper business of the traveler. The assumption here is that we should all be doing those things which are unattainable at home and not diluting the joys of foreign places.

In the words of Sadat, I wanted to take my village with me, to visit abroad in a way that made me feel at home and provided peace of mind. To do this it was essential to maintain some contact with the piano. One of the greatest pleasures to be found in travel for those who feel likewise is to enjoy the *feeling* of being someplace, really *knowing* you are someplace, and having that feeling heightened by producing music in just such unfamiliar surroundings, much as a like sentiment might be advanced by painters and writers.

The unthinking might persist in arguing that this latter sensation should be satisfied by "seeing things." However, it should be obvious that a true realization of *presence* can likely not be absorbed entirely through the eyes alone, but — and surely Spengler's criticism of the "light-world" supports this — would best be reinforced by entering the consciousness through as many senses as possible.

Laurie Lee in "A Song for Spain" from *A Rose for Winter*, captures this heightened sense of reality by describing the use of the senses in just such a way as "We entered to the cry of a fisherman . . . leaning against a huge sweating barrel. . . . We drank black wine . . . singing with a passion that shook his whole body. . . . He sang through his nose, with the high-pitched cry of Africa. . . . He reeked of wine and olives, of garlic and the sea. He reeked also of glory. . . . He inhabited still the pure sources of feeling . . . increasingly clogged by each new triumph of enlightenment and comfort."

This vividness of feeling is what we are after if we seek to play in "the great silences of the mountains and the sea," and I might add, the unknown cities, for surely they are "silent" for us as well. If we reach down into the roots of our awareness we will usually find that we are most arrested by our experiences when they are perceived through a variety of sensations such as when we are shopping for or preparing food, trodding dense, historic streets and neighborhoods, meeting foreign friends, watching good shows, or dining in ideal surroundings with congenial companions.

To these buttressed sensations of "being there," I would add the playing of a piano in a foreign place. One not only hears oneself playing in a dimensionalized, spatial setting but a time setting as well. To experience this sense of reality, which for the nonperformer may have lost its poignancy by overuse, is an easy call-up for the pianist who, through the enchantment of his playing, can summon an indelible comprehension by means of his own spellbinding.

Finding a piano on which to practice when staying in a strange city is often more daunting than finding the time to do it. Hotels can usually afford an easy solution since they generally have one or more pianos around if you can make arrangements for their use and be flexible with your hours.

With quite a few hours to kill one time at the Kahler Hotel in Rochester I sought out the person who coordinated guests' sightseeing, sports, and social activities. It turned out to be the perfect solution. While never having made piano appointments before, the lady leapt to the bait and suggested a small piano in the evening dining room. This space was abandoned during the day and stood in pitch darkness just off the lobby.

After four o'clock in the afternoon I would grope my way through the maze of tables and chairs, switch on a tiny light on the music rack, and sit down to a humble console piano to work through half a dozen pieces. Eventually more light came on and dining room employees gradually appeared with stacks of napkins and table cloths and began their setups. Near the end of my hour the room was outfitted in proper splendor, but the transition from blackness to full table settings occurred so smoothly that my playing seemed to come alive with the room itself. Moreover, I was spared any selfconsciousness by the subtle introduction of busboys and waiters over a congenial span of time.

Chapter 12

Maintaining the Piano

Elyse Mach in her book, *Great Pianists Speak for Themselves,* quotes Vladimir Horowitz as saying, "All pianos are more or less good; but they need constant care and don't often receive it. At least every month or two they should be tuned and voiced(!). If it isn't done, the piano will run down like a human being who neglects his health."

Being less sanguine than Horowitz about the multitude of exemplary instruments, I would prefer saying that, whether due to bad maintenance, attrition, or an initially meager supply, there are very few good pianos, at least that become available to the struggling amateurs of the world.

Horowitz continues, this time on a more even keel, to say, "Pianos change their timbre and tone with the weather, the atmospheric conditions, or movement. When they come from the factory, they are like a new car. You can't drive them at top speed . . . a piano has some eleven thousand parts, and if one of those goes awry, then the piano doesn't function right. A piano is very vulnerable. Generally winters are too dry and summers too wet. I have my piano tuned once a month when I am at home, whether I play it or not."

Acclimatizing the Piano

These wooden instruments are extremely sensitive to changes in weather. At no time is the trauma to its thousands of components more severe than when it is first introduced into new surroundings. In fact, if it is delivered in winter, Bechstein, in its soulful brochure on the subject, urges that the newcomer be set in its *unheated* room (tough, if it's your living room) for at least twelve hours. Only after that period should the keyboard cover be opened and heat be increased gradually over several days until the normal room temperature is reached.

Positioning the Piano

Bechstein goes on to assert that, like some precious house cat, your instrument will have its "favorite place." It will be happiest if it is not on an outside wall and not near a source of heat or humidity. It should be protected from drafts but not confined somewhere in a close niche. It wants both open space and safeguarding, perhaps a tall order in most houses.

Humidity

The relative degree of moisture in the air is the key element in determining your piano's happiness. The felicitous range is between 40 and 65 percent moisture. This can be constantly monitored by a hygrometer or psychrometer. These can be obtained through Viking Sales Co., 14630 Titus Street, Panorama City, CA 91402. These moisture readings can be modified by heating, air-conditioning, water-evaporator, and humidification.

Bechstein cautions that, "your instrument could resent this"; but whether this resentment might be occasioned by such finicky manipulation of the environment or by the extremes in humidity that caused it in the first place remains uncertain. We are further warned that, like wine, our instrument does not cope well with sudden changes in temperature, so it may be that it is the *speed* of adjustment which makes it capricious. In any event it is pretty safe to say that moderation is the byword when monkeying with the piano's environment.

Larry Fine's *Piano Book* treats this general subject of maintenance in a thorough and professional manner. Also, Lou Tasciotti has written several thorough articles on maintenance in *The Piano Quarterly*. They both represent good source material for the care of your piano. The following are some additional nuances that have occurred in my own custodianship of instruments.

Rusting Strings

If the strings show a tendency to rust, as they do in my marine-oriented region, there is only one safe way to clean them. Obtainable anywhere at supermarkets and hardware stores is the abrasive type of scouring pad that is fabricated solely of plastic materials and contains no metal or wood. Cut this into manageable 2″ × 4″ working sizes and keep these handy for an occasional cleaning. Just rub one pad gently along any rusting portions of the strings, and keep your own skin away from the metal. Use no liquids, oils, or sprays, nor any saturated pad cleaners on the strings. That's all there is to it.

Heavy rust is best removed by a professional. He is able to file it off in a laborious process where he employs more serious abrasives, including a pumice-like stone. Such energetic housekeeping can create a substantial residue of dry, powdery rust that descends onto the soundboard. When the job is completed he will blow this out with a vacuum cleaner reversed in its cycle so as to jet the air out rather than suck it in.

Open or Closed

As a precaution, any decent piano should be kept closed when not in use. A fine piano is a veritable objet d'art, which is to say it is infinitely more complex than a violin or a cello, which generally stay in their cases when they are not being played. Moreover, there is the threat of open windows and doorways and whatever they might bring. The placing of lamps, gewgaws, pictures, and bric-a-brac on the sides of the music rack will thwart any good intentions about keeping the instrument routinely closed.

Vases, cups, and glasses simply do not belong on the piano. Bechstein informs us of two truths that will not easily be gainsaid. The first is that such vessels commonly contain liquid, and the second is that they can just as commonly be knocked over. It doesn't take a genius to guess what happens when that good old sugary soft drink finds its way down into the threads of the tuning pins and further on into the holes in the pin block, not to mention the nearby metal and felt and goodness knows where else.

Keep vases, cups, and glasses away from the piano. If the craving to place a vase of flowers on the lid becomes overwhelming, fill it with artificial flowers, but never any water. I feel that the piano, much like an efficient car or boat, should be kept free of anything except the tools and equipment necessary to perform on it such as music, pens, pencils, and metronome, in order to encourage frequent cleaning, habitual maintenance, and routine closing.

Control of Moisture

Undue moisture can not only cause rust but also swollen hammers and action parts. Dryness and heat may dehydrate the pin block or even crack it and, further, cause hair-raising fissures in the soundboard. In damp regions you should obtain one of the heating elements manufactured by Dampp-Chaser. This will provide a delicate warmth from below the strings that gently permeates the wood. These come in fifteen- and twenty-five-watt strengths. In American or Japanese pianos one can be installed inside the action just over the keys. In European pianos, Horowitz correctly cautions, "The German wood cannot tolerate much change in climate." So in the case of European pianos, the five-feet-long, twenty-five-watt unit should be positioned under the action area of the soundboard and underneath the case. For dry, desert climates the same manufacturer can supply a humidistat for controlling excessive dryness.

Internal and External Covers

As further protection against rusting strings in damp regions, or when a piano is to be left for an extended period, it is possible to overlay the metal harp and strings with a cloth cover. The trick here is not to have the cover act as a blotter and actually *attract* moisture. This can be managed by ordering impregnated cloth from your jeweler of the type that is used to line silver drawers and shelves to inhibit tarnishing. One brand is called Pacific Cloth and if not readily available locally can be ordered directly from Eureka Manufacturing, 47 Elm Street, Norton, MA 02766-0917. A typical grand piano takes from three to four yards. You can fit this cover to the inside shape of the piano by first running a length in full width from the fall board down to the very end of the metal harp. Next you baste or pin a short piece parallel to protect the treble area. For thorough protection there is no need to make it formfitting. It is best to leave some gathering around the edges to help make a better seal.

To improve the appearance you can overlay this material with a lightweight suede cloth stitched to the felt along the edges thus making a double thickness. This results in a classy inner cover. The gentle heat from the Dampp-Chaser is mildly restrained from escaping upward by the nonporous plastic cover on top. So far, so good.

In an attempt to gild the lily further, I have worked with outer full piano case covers of various sorts. The stock factory covers are usually bulky, quilted affairs that seem to be designed for institutional and backstage use. They are contrived to insulate the instrument from accidents due to clumsy stagehand jostling and would doubtless help it survive a fire and an earthquake if need be. They have minimum desirability as a domestic cover.

Note the fabric on the cover of Joseph Horowitz's book, *Conversations with Arrau*. This suggests a tailored cover of lightweight navy blue or black felt with possibly a little gold piping at the corner seam around the lid and punctuated with a decorative border at the keyboard end. Your imagination can take over from there.

It is not too hard to fashion one of these yourself. You overlay the flat top lid of the piano with enough fabric to outline in chalk the outer edge of the wood all around. A skirt of about eighteen inches descends from this edge on all sides, except over the fall board where your powers as improviser and seamstress must be brought into play.

Another protective embellishment would be a traditional keyboard cloth. These are usually cut out of green, red, or blue felt and placed loosely over the keys before the fall board is closed. The exact size, except for Imperial jumbo concert keyboards, is around $5\frac{1}{2}''$ × $50''$ with the edges neatly pinked. The weight for the felt is approximately twelve to fourteen ounces.

Tuning

Frequency of tuning for us amateurs, Maestro Horowitz notwithstanding, should be planned at least every three months with thorough voicing, called "toning" in Europe, about once a year. This last is vitally important. We have discussed the over-hardening of hammers where brilliance is increased to a crystal-shattering peak. This phenomenon can occur naturally in older pianos when the hammer felt has become over-compacted. It is a devilish job to revoice an entire instrument when these felts become solidified like ball peen hammers. It is for this reason that Tasciotti recommends that some voicing be done at each tuning visit.

When hammers reach this hardened state it is often necessary to file off the tops of all the hammers with a rasp, reshape them, and start hand-pricking each hammer with a voicing prong and thus matching and blending them all from scratch. Tasciotti suggests that a piano receiving six to eight hours of use a day should have its hammers filed once a year. Thus, two hours of use a day would indicate a filing every third year. This is an act of high talent for a good technician wherein great restraint and artfulness are called for.

Voicing

Very often a piano will be judged to lack brilliance in the treble and authority and warmth throughout the middle range. The tried and true antidote for this lack of singing tone is to lacquer the hammers or "juice" them, as the rather obscene expression goes. By applying a liquid hardening agent to the felt, the hammer mass becomes solidified and enables the technician to resoften and blend the individual mallets by pricking the felt until he achieves the sought-after tone.

The trouble arises in this process when the strings and piano are not capable of producing a full, prolonged tone in and of themselves. This singing potential can be rather easily evaluated merely by plucking the strings like a guitar with one's fingernail, being sure that the notes are "open" and undamped.

If tone decay is rapid, no amount of hardening will yield more than a metallic "ping." It is essential, therefore, that this talent for sustaining a rich, lengthy tone be verified at the very outset of one's involvement with any piano. A talented instrument is one where absolute contact exists between the string and the bridge and where that perfect marriage transfers to the soundboard to produce a heavenly resonance. No amount of hardening, shaping, or "juicing" hammers will alone assure a fuller and warmer tone.

Alfred Brendel in *Musical Thoughts and Afterthoughts* makes a significant point about voicing when he says, "[the technician's] usual test for evenness of tone is to drop the arm strongly and separately on each key. . . . [T]his is of little use in detecting the subtle distinctions needed in voicing. It does not lead to evenness in the *piano* or *pianissimo* range." These last references are of course to volume.

He proposes taking the piano *legato*, that is a soft, singing touch as one's starting point: "since that is when you need evenness and *not* in heavily accented forte playing where the difference in level intended from one note to the other may well carry the ear across any unintentional accents caused by unsatisfactory voicing."

However, in running this thought by my own technician, he said that voicing must be sensitive not only to both percussive and legato playing, but that it must satisfy the soft pedal shift to fewer unison strings as well. Additionally, it should be undertaken with the piano in its customary state of openness or closedness as the case may be. Voicing is a complicated art, particularly when you realize that the prong is inserted low on the hammer to soften tones and higher up near the crown to intensify tone.

My technician complained to me recently that he had been under the gun to restring entirely an almost new piano. A previous technician had sprayed the strings with a popular metal lubricant and preservative. The spray had slightly deadened the steel strings and, much worse, had intruded into the coilings of the wound bass strings and thus muffled the bass range of the piano as if it were permanently dampered. Moreover, since he had sprayed the whole length of all of the strings, some of the liquid had insidiously seeped down into the screw portion of the tuning pins and into the hardwood pin block where slippage caused the pins not to hold their tune. That technical miscreant claimed to have treated dozens of pianos in that identical manner, thus escalating his crime up to plague proportions. You can see, therefore, the value of aligning yourself with a reliable technician who will treat your instrument with the respect, knowledge, and loving care that it deserves.

Your technician will have some further tricks up his sleeve for improving your piano's tone within realistic limits. He will naturally see that all strings are "seated" in order to be sure that their vibrations are being faithfuly transmitted through the bridge to the soundboard. This he accomplishes by tapping them solidly down on to the bridge to relieve any possible binding on the edges of the pins.

He may try "turning" a string if that is called for. This is the act of rotating one by twisting it to see if he can coax a further resonance from it.

Periodically he will check all the regulatory refinements such as after-touch, hammer let-off, key dip, knuckle articulation, or down pressure. In the end he should summarize what remains to be done so at the very least you can plan ahead for the time when you wish to lavish a little more affection on your instrument.

Cosmetics

Most manufacturers recommend cleaning the wood surfaces with only a dry, soft duster or cloth. If film develops the cloth can be moistened slightly and will usually remove any buildup of dirt. In stubborn cases, Bösendorfer suggests a very mild mixture of water and Ivory Liquid, in which case they say to wipe clean with two different dry, soft rags. If available, Nequiars Plastic Polish MGH-10 can also be used to maintain the high sheen of polyester. This should be applied with a soft foam pad, allowed to dry, then wiped off with the trusty soft, clean rag.

Ivory or plastic keys should come clean with a damp towel. Purists may be inclined to use milk on the ivory as a form of soul food.

Repairs to the Case

Repairing dings and abrasions on the high-sheen polyester wood cases has always required a laborious two trips to the customer's house. Bösendorfer has perfected a polyester repair material that sets up rapidly enough in twenty or thirty minutes for the finish technician to accomplish the work in one trip. This is good news for high-gloss owners who want to keep their instruments in first-class condition. Most technicians have access to this panacea through their supply wholesaler or Kimball of America.

Chapter 13

Extra Piano Uses
and Improvisation

Duets Played on One Piano

So far we have dealt only with the player's own relationship with the piano. It has been a solo affair. Yet, submitting to, and coordinating with, the musical prerogatives of others is a known catalyst for accelerating reading skills and sharpening one's ear. This is not to leave out the element of pure pleasure. The simplest form this group music-making can take is the duet: pieces written for one piano and four hands.

There is a rich literature available for this combination, most of it growing out of the piano's century-old history of providing entertainment for members of the family in their home. It breaks down fundamentally into original compositions in duet form and transcriptions from existing instrumental works, or expansion of pieces written for solo piano—a form of transcription.

The most highly regarded and prolific composers of original duet material were Mozart and Schubert. The cornerstone of any duet library would have to include the works of these two composers over and above anything else. Most major music publishers offer the one volume of Mozart and two or more of Schubert. Thus launched, the duet library should be fleshed out with the Brahms Waltzes and Hungarian Dances, Debussy's "Petite Suite," Fauré's "Dolly," along with some Schumann, all following in close order. Also, many single pieces are shown in the catalogues of Carl Fischer and others. You should explore this exciting field and realize the potential for the occasion when you are fortunate enough to have another pianist on hand. The hardest part is generally conceded to be the "Primo" or

162

left side portion, although the "Secundo" or right keyboard part is the most fun, being most involved with the melody and rapid passage work. So be guided by the relative abilities of yourself and your keyboard mate.

While favoring original compositions, I like the Brahms String Quartet arrangements for one piano and four hands. They are available through Dover Press and are beautifully transcribed. Beethoven, Haydn, Mahler, Stravinsky and Tchaikovsky symphonies are to be had as well, to name only a limited part of this bountiful repertoire.

Ensemble playing needs to be taken at a slower tempo to begin with, for the obvious reason that there are the weaknesses of two people to consider. Speed can usually be picked up quickly as both players familiarize themselves with the notes and phrasing. Elbows will occasionally be bumped and hands interlocked as part of normal business. As in the case of dancing, this latter phenomenon was doubtless one of the reasons for the domestic popularity and romantic potential of this musical form.

The main thing to remember is to emphasize strong beats, usually the first and the third. Pursue them with a vengeance. Count out rests of more than one measure as, "*one,* two, three; *two,* two three; *three,* two, three," etc. Help each other with rests and dynamics. Do not be afraid to signal entrances by a forward motion of the body. Count out loud when things seem murky and indecisive. Slow movements are often tricky because of lengthy rests, spasmodic contributions, and complex accompanying rhythms. Just as John McEnroe does in tennis doubles, someone should captain the duet effort, even if you trade off. A little leadership will help immeasurably.

Always try to push your final performance over the boundaries of safe, sound conservative playing onto a more risky and challenging plane. Go into orbit, and know the thrill of an exhilarating ensemble effort. Let the chips fall where they may.

Bookspan and Yockey write that André Previn played transcriptions of the Beethoven Symphonies with his father at a very early age. This activity probably accounted for his rapid development as a skilled sight-reader. Furthermore, that persistent rehashing of transcribed symphonies no doubt guided him to an early understanding of this seminal composer's works.

I have a special fondness for Mozart's Fugue in duet form and also the charm of Debussy's "Petite Suite." Schubert's "Fantasy in F Minor," Opus 103, is a particularly haunting, epic-scale work that is not as difficult as it is emotionally demanding. It was used effectively in the film *Madame Souzatska* to reinforce the symbiotic relationship between teacher and pupil. Some of these duet pieces will remind you of the dubious sensation of downing a dose of castor oil when you start out, but stick with them. The rewards are out there.

Owning Two Pianos, or the "Harem" Syndrome

To the old saw, "He who owns two houses loses his mind; he who has two women loses his soul," we should add, "But he who has two pianos gains a friend."

One of the highly enjoyable but unheralded, nonensemble aspects of having two pianos in one's home is the sheer joy for the solo player of experiencing a change of mode in practicing and playing. Surely there are people who keep two cars in their garage who have less of an excuse than this. The situation is not unlike dining in different locales in the same house, a balcony, a terrace, a garden, a breakfast room, nook, dining room, or fireplace hearth. Moreover, the time of day and the mood and commitment of the pianist enter the picture, not to mention the variety inherent in the instruments themselves. In fact, perfectly matched pianos, while being desirable for public performance can defeat our purpose in the home if it is one of variety. One can conceive of a beautiful marriage sanctified in heaven between a big, warm, 7'6" Hamburg Steinway "C" (almost the outside limit for a residence) and a daintier 6'7" Bösendorfer, a 6'2" Blüthner, or Bechstein. This could be sheer delight, though with life being what it is, the likelihood of a house and a budget all permitting this to happen is doubtful in the extreme. But if it ever becomes possible, enjoy this fortuitous pairing no matter what it is and recognize it for what it is, a divine circumstance.

The definitive source book for the owner of two pianos is Maurice Hinson's *Music for More Than One Piano*. Besides a complete and well-organized listing of all composers and their relevant compositions, it contains lists of representatives of foreign publishers in the United States, addresses, and works including other instruments.

Performing with Others

Two-Piano Duets

Two-piano material falls into a bit of a vacuum from the standpoint of composer and publisher. More often than not such material is created, or has been created, by two performers' needs rather than something a composer or publisher viewed as having a worthwhile market. The ratio of titles is about two to one of single versus double piano duet works. Yet most of the big orchestral compositions find their way to the piano in this form. Certainly all concertos, quintets (strings plus piano, that is), anything featuring solo piano with chamber group or orchestra must devolve at the extreme to the two-piano form. Beethoven, Brahms, Chopin, Liszt, Mendelssohn, Mozart, and Schumann — these important composers are all represented in this interesting form. If you are purist, here is a case where matched pianos and a big room are most desirable.

Again, Carl Fischer obliges, along with International Music Publishers, in furnishing us with superb lists of original compositions and transcriptions for two pianos. Not surprisingly there is far less original material for two persons playing two pianos than a single instrument. Understandably, as we move out of the home, as would usually be the case, into larger and more public circumstances involving two instruments, the whole nature of the repertoire is altered. Music performed on two instruments more often is a reduction of a composition of larger form than expansion of a solo piece as in the case of simple duets.

Accompanying Others

This brings us to the matter of accompanying a vocalist or instrumentalist or group of performers. Here, as in the case of duet playing, do not hang back. Seize any opportunity to play with others of reasonable capabilities, as long as they are not in a hopeless backwater of your interests. While "pop" music is certainly not the same as serious jazz music, an admirable zeal for expanding our musical horizons should be sufficiently powerful to topple any ivory tower of snobbishness and permit us to accompany a friend who can sing but lacks a background for a ballad. Be a sport. Great pianists can play jazz, improvise, compose, and accompany someone in almost any vein. Why shouldn't you? You will advance your own efforts multifold by having to coordinate and advance with an ensemble. Moreover, the art of good accompaniment implies some exposure to the improvisatory impulse. At the very least the supporting pianist must provide an introduction, possibly an interlude of some kind, adjustments of tempo, allowance for ritards, the filling in of any lacuna, and to help bring down the house at the finale. It is one short step more to improvise on your own.

Mechanical practice keyboards are still occasionally seen in shops carrying used pianos. They tend to look like small versions of the old rectangular pianos without all the strings and soundboard. They are not especially light and are totally unsuited for travel. Their chief attribute is to silence your practice efforts and to provide a fair simulation of the action and resistance of a standard piano keyboard.

Electronic Exotica

Here might be brought up — and as quickly dismissed — the subject of combining a harpsichord or electronic keyboard with the basic piano. This surely gets into the area of novelty or, possibly, gimmicky public performance. If amusement is the only objective, the very fact that there is no significant body of literature nor any recognized historic discipline or study or consistent performance history for this combination forces us to disregard such foibles and leave them to performers in cocktail bars. A vigorous pursuit of the piano by a dedicated amateur should leave precious little time or ambition for such flotsam and jetsam.

There is, however, one electronic area that needs to be explored. It is the use of electronic keyboards when occupying a small apartment, traveling, or practicing in a remote location or practicing where a piano simply will not fit: say, on a boat, or too close to others you might disturb. A recent article in *The Piano Quarterly* by the knowledgeable George Litterst pointed out the vast number of keyboards from which the pianist has to choose. The two that seemed most like the piano were the Midiboard from Kurzweil, and the KX88 from Yamaha, to which we might add the 300 RD from Roland. All of these "controllers," as they are called, have eighty-eight keys with weighted action but *no sound* except through headphones. To produce room sound you have to get an expander module and connect them to the auxiliary input of your stereo system as you would a CD or tape deck. The cost of the digital keyboard itself is around $2,000. A further sophistication is the addition of a "Sequencer," which lets you record and edit the piano sounds you originate on the keyboard. If that were not enough, you could progress on to synthesizer effects and so on. Not only is such technical hyperbole beyond the realm of this book but it freights the already heavy burden of our piano commitment beyond reason.

While electronic keyboards, as stated previously, are outside the scope of this book, more and more pianists of jazz, pop, and rock are using them along with conventional pianos. Composers utilize them along with synthesizers and pianos as part of the creative process. In fact, unless their work is centered around the piano, they are more apt, after a period of time, to eliminate the real instrument and do all the composing with electronics. After all, if you are conceiving instrumentally there is nothing sacred about the percussive notes sounded on a piano. What does a mechanical piano action have in common with a string section other than tonality?

The leading edge of this activity might be exemplified by Oscar Peterson. In his home and sometimes on television programs, along with his ever present Bösendorfer, he employs the ultimate in musical computers, a Synclavier, manufactured by New England Digital. This tidy little rig tips the economic scales at upward of $250,000. The television demonstration of this equipment revealed that it could do virtually anything with the musical stimuli fed into it. Whole orchestras and choruses can be built up by one element at a time. This input can be altered, changed, edited, graphically notated, printed out as music, and replayed on programmable instruments or the synthesizer in an infinite stream of music-making functions. It is nice to know that they make Rolls-Royces, Aston-Martins, and Ferraris even if we don't intend to buy them. So much for the truly exotic. Now how about exotic music?

Different Types of Music

Ragtime as a Liberating Device

A precursor of contemporary American music, this seemingly primitive form of folk music embodies a greater sophistication than appears on the surface. One of the publishers of Scott Joplin's works states that Debussy commented favorably on ragtime music. Stravinsky and Gottschalk embellished the form.

For the amateur piano enthusiast, these compositions pose an immense variety of attractions:

- High entertainment value for performer and audience
- Excellent sight-reading material
- Wide dynamic range
- Delicate fingering requirement
- A rock-solid rhythm demand
- Visceral base line with good harmonic leading
- Demand for convincing phrasing
- Similarity to baroque first-beat emphasis
- Exciting syncopated melody notes
- Chance for "agogic" accents the phrasing
- Requisite loose, relaxed approach
- Relief from the standard classical repertoire
- Brevity
- Fun

Who could ask for anything more? In fact, these rags could make peculiar but oddly related bedfellows of the essential Chopin Waltzes. Why? Chiefly because they make comparable demands and supply comparable rewards for the performer. We have only to compare a few measures of Chopin's Waltz in A-flat, Opus 34, No. 1

with Joplin's quite similar feeling in "Harmony Club Waltz."

The Joplin rags I find most edifying in order of preference are:
- "Easy Winners"
- "Sunflower Slow Drag"
- "Cascades"
- "Elite Syncopation"
- "Maple Leaf Rag"
- "Ragtime Dance"

Closely related to the rags, although rarely thought of in this jazz/classical context, would be the tangos of Brazil. If proof were needed, look to the fine rendition of a select group of these composed by Ernesto Nazareth and performed by Arthur Moreira Lima on Pro-Art CD. Moreover, at the commemoration of the 500,000th Steinway piano at Carnegie Hall in 1988, Feghali played Nazareth's "Odeon" to a delighted audience. In his post-performance speech he said to nobody's surprise, "He was our Scott Joplin." It is charming but almost impossible to find due to copyright technicalities in Brazil.

Jazz as a Backup to Classical Study

My feeling about the relevance of jazz and jazz improvisation to classical study is that it can be the most highly specific of almost any area of support. The reason is that throughout the evolution of jazz from Dixieland on up through Swing, to Rhythm and Blues, progressive, Rock, and fusion, there are only certain of its meanderings that seem to be productive in the study of classical piano. For example, it is hard to see the value of the unrelieved hyperdynamics and simplistic harmonies of Dixieland, Boogie-Woogie, or Rock, or the smarmy insinuations of bossa nova, pop, or disco.

Yet if we seek just the right forms of jazz to study and enjoy, we can stimulate and reinforce our serious piano study. After quality ragtime I would have to emphasize the ultimate right-hand and free-flight direction of the Tatum/Peterson school, and eventually come to rest on such accessible progressive work of players like Bud Powell and Billy Taylor. These composer/performers carry mere facile improvisation high up into that rarefied atmosphere where an entirely new composition is fashioned from the old. Complex, "layered" harmonies of the eleventh and thirteenth mix company with melodies that overflow their banks and beguilingly deceive rather than lock themselves into diatonic certainty.

Examples of jazz precursors in classical literature of the piano generally are topped by the glittering third variation of the second movement of Beethoven's Sonata in C minor, Opus 111, about which Tovey says, "[paraphrase] its difficulties can be mastered with practice whereas the 106 ("Hammerklavier") is the virtuoso class and defies interpretation by the amateur player."

The story of discovering the roots of the jazz piano idiom by looking backward through the centuries does not stop there by any means. One of the reasons why the Beethoven example has been pointed to in fairly recent piano commentary of the 1940s and 1950s is because of its linkage with the so-called swing rhythm of the 1930s and 1940s. As has been meticulously pointed out in books and articles on the subject, this swing rhythm was ordinarily notated as follows:

while it was actually played more to this academic notation:

Now comes Beethoven who wrote this:

"Ah ha!" you might say. "Dotted rhythms don't swing." The precedent for these triplet leanings can be traced back to Baroque music where, as in the case of Bach's Partita No. 6, and numerous other examples, the intent was to disregard the confinement of dotted notation and adopt a rolling triplet rhythm. This difference can be heard in performance by comparing a recording of the scholarly Schnabel, Serkin, or Brendel to a more modern Ashkenazy, Bishop, or Pollini; or the recorded performance of a scholarly Schnabel or Serkin compared to a more modern Ashkenazy or Bishop.

Jazz writers of the 1940s and 1950s struggled through a period of notational dilemma during which they tried to show this swing or "leaning" of the eighth notes by dotted patterns. If rendered literally this would play no more like the feeling intended than straight eighth notes would; neither described accurately the way they were supposed to be played. Actually in the final Adagio movement of Opus 111, this particular "jazz" variation stems from the original triplet configuration in 9/16 time that makes the later emphasis quite clear. It is hard to think of a better textbook example of how so-called swing rhythm is at variance with the written notes that have come to be used in attempting to transcribe it in writing. Despite either the dotted eighth and sixteenth notation or the simplified eighth-note shortcut, the modern pianist should generally adhere to the triplet feeling Beethoven so adequately wrote down. He is, to put it very simply, supposed to "swing."

From Charlie Parker's time on, much of that traditional swing rhythm has been more or less modified in serious jazz improvisation. From the 1960s to the present it is more the case that the rhythm *has* evened out and tended to conform more literally to the eighth-note reading, having lost much of its triplet feeling that characterized swing. Jazz over the last twenty-five years has moved ahead and utilized more diverse means of syncopation, such as often accenting on weak beats or between beats, doubling up in spirited surges, complicating the harmonies, heightening importance of phrasing, exploiting the omission of diatonic resolution, and experimenting with elaborate and complex melodic departures and paraphrases.

Furthermore, this new jazz tends not only to introduce more involved harmonies of the ninth, eleventh, and thirteenth, but indulges in subtle alternative quasi-enharmonic and chromatic chordings in order to stray further from the original harmonies but still convey the overall spirit and forward motion of a piece. They achieved this by a devious route similar to that of an impressionist painting. These sequences of harmonies, perhaps because they are changes from the

original as well as chords, came to be known as changes. If we had
Beethoven with us today and willing to appear on a talk show, we
would be quizzing him not about his sequence of chords but about
his "changes," and he would doubtless be way ahead of us in snappy
rebuttal.

The strong beats of a measure, as much as possible, have come
to be considered poor resting places for notes of fundamental triads,
especially since we are no longer concerned about where to sing
"June" and "Moon," or shouldn't be anyway. In modern jazz improvisation, the desired melodic or improvisational line attempts to
take refuge in the mordent or nonconclusive passing note of strong
beats. This way the resolution of both harmony and melody is de-
ferred *as long as possible.* It is sometimes never allowed to rest until
the end of the piece, if even then. Put another way, harmonies are
kept rich, oblique, and slightly out of focus, and melodies elusive and
not wholly predictable.

This brings us to our standard solo repertoire and examples of
compositions that contain some of this idiom of current jazz phrasing
and construction. We do not need to look far for this harmonic and
melodic seedbed.

Jazz and Keyboard Workshop (September 1987) pointed out
similarities between Chopin's Etude in A minor, Opus 25, No. 4,
with its potential offbeat alternation between hands to sight, as an
important precursor of the left-hand anticipatory style of jazz great
Errol Garner.

There were also present some suspended, aggressive melody
notes that helped to foster an attitude of tension until harmonic
resolution was permitted to take place at long last.

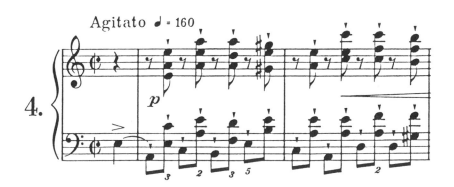

Chopin's Scherzo in the second movement of Sonata No. 3 fits this mode of comparison by employing a series of melodic syncopations against a ¾ time signature.

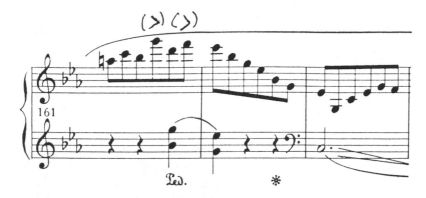

The avoidance of principal harmonic triad tones on strong beats is aided by rhythmic syncopation and jazz-like phrasing or "blown" melody lines by referring to Chopin's formidable Prelude in B-flat minor, Opus 28, No. 16, a virtuoso work:

This same employment of a soaring single note line occurs again in the Berceuse. You have only to slow down the Prelude and to speed up the last part of the Berceuse and kick in an imaginary string bass in your head. Now by playing both at a moderate jazz clip you can recognize the similarity between Chopin's line and that of Peterson and many jazz performers today.

This whole matter of improvising is gone into more thoroughly in the worthy *Jazz and Keyboard Workshop*. It is a useful tool for informing yourself about what is happening in modern jazz piano. More to the point is their fundamental approach to the subject, which often brings to light the connection between great classical composers and great modern improvisers. Scriabin and Chopin references have been made in recent issues together with relevant ethnic composers. (Inquiries to the *Jazz and Keyboard Workshop* can be addressed to P.O. Box 933, Paramus, NJ 07653-9948.)

The object here is to show a way to use another medium for studying difficult material and bringing it to heel. The jazz comparison is merely another weapon in your arsenal for attacking advanced piano works; the theory being that we need all the help we can get.

Chapter 14

Books and Other Publications

Books

The subject of the piano contends with cooking, antiques, and travel as a wellspring of endless books aimed at the listener, the amateur, and the near professional. Most of the books fit into these broad categories of straight reference, biographical/interview, and instructive.

Straight references would include dictionaries, record catalogues, *Grove's Dictionary of Music and Musicians* and other encyclopedias, music catalogues, lists of pieces for the repertoire, rankings according to difficulty, piano construction, etc.

Biographies are about a single composer or performer, largely anecdotal, often including lists of works performed on records. These would include *Interviews and Anthologies of Interviews* which would comprise single or multiple discussions with artists and can be informative and instructive, particularly in the hands of a sophisticated interviewer and if there is a good index.

Performance oriented books of a reasonably high level can be essential to the sincere and dedicated amateur and are a great source for repertoire ideas and development. This would include *"How to"* texts of instruction which can be effective up to the highest levels of playing but must be geared to your grade or plateau.

This chapter includes a bibliography of titles that are both instructive and pleasurable to read in conjunction with one's playing, with comments on each of them. However, there is a small, indispensable group of books that should never be more than an arm's length from the keyboard. It should consist of:

1. *Dictionary of Music.* Harvard, Harper's or similar
2. *Music for the Piano.* Friskin and Freundlich

3. *The Literature of the Piano.* Hutcheson
4. *Piano Music of Six Great Composers.* Ferguson
5. *Beethoven Sonatas.* Craxton and Tovey

1. The need for a dictionary is obvious. While it may seem that a familiarity with the usual Italian terms of *allegro, tempi,* and *expressivo* is adequate and that some understanding of cognates will see you through, such is not the case. These markings and directions constitute too rich and complex a trove of musical support to stint. As an example, consider that a ritardando in French music is *"Cedez."* Unless the music itself suggests a ritard, without knowledge of the term, the word may well be meaningless. Dictionaries by Harvard (edited by Willi Apel) and Harper's (edited by Christine Ammer) are both good. Moreover, the dictionaries contain much other pertinent information like long lists of basic sonatas, historical information, Köchel numbers for Mozart, and on and on. Any conscientious amateur, at whatever grade, needs a musical dictionary.

2. *Music for the Piano,* by James Friskin and Irwin Freundlich is a rich goldmine of brief descriptions of most of the music you will ever want to play. Terse, direct comments on degree of difficulty and specific trouble areas accompany all significant entries. The authors are harsh and opinionated in everything they write. The comprehensiveness and format of the book are its principal assets. The hundreds of crisp judgments are right to the point, and while some of them are outdated or arguable, the work as a whole is a valuable companion that will likely see daily use.

3. *The Literature of the Piano,* by Ernest Hutcheson (updated by Rudolph Ganz) also covers the principal body of piano solo work but with considerably more attention to the works you are more likely to want to study. Proportionately more space is devoted to more popular and worthy selections. There is much more depth, and it is more useful for shaping the entire repertoire; that is, it is less of a catalogue, which the Friskin book tends to be.

This work would be most helpful in deciding which sonata at which level of difficulty would be appropriate, given a specific composer's group. Along with the increased length of the descriptions, there flows much more comment on interpretation and other performance details.

4. *Piano Music of Six Great Composers,* by Donald Ferguson, as the title suggests, further narrows the field down to Beethoven, Schubert, Schumann, Chopin, Brahms, and Debussy. Considering

its forty-year age, it is still a gem of a book. He treats the works of these few great composers so elaborately from the performer's viewpoint, that had he included Bach and Liszt we might have designated this as the dominant manual of performance for life. Nevertheless, prize it for what it is, an invaluable "open sesame" to the essential works of these six cornerstone composers.

5. *Beethoven Sonatas,* edited by Harold Craxton and Donald Francis Tovey, comes in three volumes of music published by the Associated Board in London. Despite the slightly antiquated notational styling and extraneous markings, the music volumes themselves are worth their weight in Steinways for Tovey's explanatory text that precedes every one of the thirty-one sonatas. I find it irresistible not to include some examples of this commentary:

- "Persons who hit the top E smartly, as with a thimble, had better leave music and music-lovers in peace." (Opus 2, No. 2)
- (Following a technical suggestion to simplify). "The Slough of Despond and the Serbonian Bog will be drained before all such possibilities are exhausted." (Opus 7)
- "The people who 'understand' great music beforehand will never see anything in it except a mirror of their own minds. The player who obeys orders faithfully will be constantly discovering their real meaning." (Opus 10, No. 3)
- "If people still exist who do not see the point of a pianissimo arpeggio without pedal...why consider their interests?" (ibid.)
- "Play all Beethoven's repeats...you are playing a peaceful dance for gracious souls that deserve their leisure — not imparting information to busy people who do not want to waste time in hearing twice what their stenographers have already noted and filed." (Opus 31, No. 3)
- "No criticism is so mean and mischievous as that which discourages young players from playing great music accurately because 'correctness is not enough.' Who supposes it is?" (Opus 110)
- "...personal preferences do not affect questions of what Beethoven wrote...you need no fear that you may cramp your own personality by attending to [his] wishes. Beethoven's mind is very large and infinite in its variety; which the minds of people who are confident in their ability to correct and improve him are very small and exactly alike." (Opus 31, No. 3)

Bravo!

Similar gems in infinite variety accompany each and every sonata. Do not be confused by Tovey's other publication, *A Companion to Beethoven's Pianoforte Sonatas*, which is a proper book and just as instructive, though along more scholarly lines, being more in the style of a textbook rather than stimulating notes written to inspire the performer sitting right at the keyboard. Also the texts are different. Be content with acquiring those sonatas, if only for the text.

There the list becomes slightly diffused. If the task were to select only five piano books with which to be cast away on a desert island along with a decent Steinway B, a tuning wrench, voicing prong, and a full trunk of music, these would be the titles I would choose, with perhaps the dictionary to sit on.

The earlier expression relating to the reference books, "within arm's reach" was not intended figuratively, it meant literally *within arm's reach!* Often the questions that arise about degree of difficulty, execution, fingering, dynamics, composer's intentions, performance, popularity over the years, key selection and the rest, come up right on the spot when you are practicing and do not crave a major interruption.

I recently attempted to sight-read Schumann's "Fantasie in C," and I was caught off guard by the challenge inherent in the formidable second movement, particularly by the rapid martial dotted rhythms, to mention only one of several hurdles. I wound up in such a state of frustration that I whipped open Ferguson's *Six Composers* book, knowing he had a lot to say on Schumann, and on page 167 found the following: "One who seeks a cure for spiritual paralysis should subject himself to the middle movement of this 'Fantasie'. It is a March . . . but driven by an exaltation impossible to be enacted by mortal feet." I was sufficiently soothed to think of trying that impossible march another time.

This second rank of books is both pleasurable and useful for the amateur pianist. While not needed within the famous arm's reach, they serve the armchair musician as H. V. Morton and Jan Morris serve the traveler, and Julia Child and M. F. K. Fisher the cook.

Bernstein, Seymour, *With Your Own Two Hands*, New York, NY: G. Schirmer, 1981. This is a more generalized approach that could apply to any endeavor where one would acquire knowledge for its own sake, much as Gallwey's *Inner Tennis* can reach into the musical performance field. Such psychological barriers as "controlled tension" are discussed, along with many specific technical problems, even such far-afield topics as drugs, the choosing of friends, and that good breathing.

Bodky, Erwin, *The Interpretation of Bach's Keyboard Works*, Cambridge, Mass.: Harvard University Press, 1960. This definitive reference for Bach is complete with tempos for all movements of every single work, not to mention articulation according to the proper baroque disciplines. Certainly more is contained here than the amateur will need to know on the subject, especially if time is set aside for that other representative of the sixteenth century, Domenico Scarlatti. Still, points covered are invaluable for anyone wanting to get to the bottom of this master's works.

Brendel, Alfred, *Musical Thoughts and Afterthoughts*, Princeton, NJ: Princeton University Press, 1976. Brendel writes very well. His slim volume brims with Beethoven, Schubert, and Liszt material. A fascinating dividend is a highly informative chapter on "Coping with Pianos." It relates in detail his own methods of handling instruments and technicians and is very valuable on its own. It may come as a shock that he voices his own instrument, but our amateur should have his hands full enough to be entitled to shirk that task. Remember that Slough of Despond.

Cooke, Charles, *Playing the Piano for Pleasure*, New York, NY: Simon and Schuster, 1941. In the same expansive breath this little gem by Cooke, himself a former staff writer of long standing with *The New Yorker*, has something in it for everyone. Slanted at the lower level one-half hour a day amateur, it is nonetheless able to be appreciated and enjoyed by anyone committed to playing the piano regularly, primarily because of its polished, anecdotal style.

Huneker, James, *Chopin: The Man and His Music*, New York, NY: Dover Publications, 1966. Here we have detailed descriptions of all the composer's works. In addition to being a famed novelist, Huneker was a music student (in Paris) and a music critic. Combining a writer's talent with a musician's ear, we are given here a rare verbalization of multiple artistic works by this ultimate composer for the piano. The detailing of all the compositions makes delightful, even poetic, reading, which should stir the fervent amateur to greater heights.

Kentner, Louis, *Piano*, New York, NY: Schirmer Books, 1976. Kentner's book with its simplistic title is a good broad-brush approach to the entire subject in an inviting format, beginning right with the construction of the instrument and carrying on through to final performance. To accomplish this in a digestible package he has wisely concentrated on three greats, Bach, Chopin, and Liszt. It is a good support book, not perhaps earmarked for the desert island, but worthy of a lengthy stay somewhere near your piano.

Lockwood, Albert, *Notes on the Literature of the Piano*, New York, NY: Da Capo Press, 1968. This book cannot hold a candle to Hutcheson's. It is more of a glorified listing of pieces and suffers from acute hardening of the arteries. Endless outmoded composers are included with more encyclopedic than selective intent. The brief passages about composers in which we have continuing interest are choked with often abrasive opinions that are themselves half outmoded. Still, with all of that, here and there are some very significant thoughts that can serve to flesh out one's own full-blown concept of a work. Moreover, some of his pronouncements have endured as gospel, having been prophetic when they were written in the early part of this century. This endures as more of an historical document of interest to pianists than as an essential library addition.

Matthews, Dennis, *Keyboard Music*, Newton Abbey, Devon: David and Charles, 1972. Matthews's book, a collection of essays, contains an abundance of readable material on all periods, along with a particularly rich treatment of Schumann and other Romantics by John Ogden. This work is really *about* piano music and how it evolved but is rewarding for what it can relate to the pianist about his own repertoire and study choices.

Morhange-Motchane, Marthe, *Thematic Guide to Piano Literature*, New York, NY: G. Schirmer, 1982–88. These five volumes set forth *all* themes of *all* movements of *all* works by Bach (in this case, unfortunately, lacking the suites), Handel, Mozart, Beethoven, Chopin, Mendelssohn, Schubert, Schumann, and Liszt. Furthermore, these works are *all* graded by *each* movement as to degree of difficulty: intermediate, difficult, advanced, etc.

It could be quibbled that the Chopin Etude in Sixths (Opus 25, No. 8) is less difficult than the Etude in Thirds (Opus 25, No. 6), these being ranked similarly by the editor; but this is small potatoes. A serious ranking by any qualified professional is a lot better than nothing at all and can, as in this work, be exceedingly useful and well presented. Another book containing Brahms and another of Debussy and Ravel would complete this ensemble and make it sparkle, but our cup already runneth over.

Newman, William S., *The Pianist's Problems*, New York, NY: Harper and Row, 1974. This fine and prolific writer on keyboard matters concentrates here on the "how to" approach, including practice, performance, and numerous helpful hints and suggestions. It is an excellent book that is well worth keeping and underlining, and linking up very well with the Charles Cooke volume. There is much emphasis here about not playing over your mistakes and so on, but the form these bromides takes is skillfully arranged and entertainingly described. Also, there is an excellent list of source references in the back of the book running to several pages.

Newman, William S., *Performance Practices in Beethoven's Piano Sonatas*, London: J. M. Dent and Sons, 1971. This book is compelling and scholarly, though not so fundamental to the amateur's needs as in the case of Tovey's Sonata notes. While it owes some fleshiness to oft-repeated material and photos about ancient pianos, the exhibit breaking down all movements of the thirty-two Sonatas is useful along with a lot of performance tips and examples.

Slenczynska, Ruth, *Music at Your Fingertips*, Garden City, NY: Doubleday, 1961. I speculate as to what demon possessed the publisher to let fly with this superb little volume and not include an index. The point in this case is that Slenczynska took the problem approach to her suject by tying in and relating the various difficulties that are encountered in attempting to master various standard works. Admirable. How much easier it would be to use this book effectively if only the index were available.

Incidentally, more than half of the indices that managed to be printed are worse than nothing when it comes to specifying the composer's individual works. Such indexing as the following is an abomination:

> Chopin, F. 90–4, 110, 120, 123, 124, 138, 145, 189, 302, 305, 412, 586f.

Obviously such listings should look like this:

> Chopin, F.
>   Ballades, Op. 23 (G minor), 220
>   Op. 38 (F minor), 223
>   Op. 47 (A-flat Major), 224, etc.

Bear in mind that to transform an otherwise useful book into a true reference it is worth taking the time to create your index of composers and their works; it is not as time consuming as you would think since you need only index those items for which you have the greatest interest.

Whiteside, Abby, *Mastering the Chopin Etudes and Other Essays,* New York, NY: Prentice-Hall, 1947. Abby Whiteside's analysis of the Etudes could have been as seminal as its title. A bit clumsy and fuzzy, it could have benefited from a skilled editor and an index. Making due allowance for its sometimes awkward structure, this is an excellent book. It ties in much of the philosophy of Tobias Matthay and others as related to the performance of these seminal studies. Despite some hobbling demerits and its shambling style, there is valuable instruction in these joyless pages.

Here we come to that tertiary stratum of books that is so enjoyable for the piano enthusiast to read. They are written about the piano and those who excel at playing it. Some are devoted to single composers. Others are collected interviews, often conducted by a premier pianist or teacher. They belong in every amateur's library, or at least on the shelves of the library he frequents. Some deal with one concert performer, some with many. Most useful from a reference standpoint are those that boast a thorough index by composers *and* their works.

Chase, Mildred Portney, *Just Being at the Piano.* Berkeley, CA: Creative Arts, 1985. This is another encouraging and inspirational book like *A Soprano on Her Head,* and *Tone Deaf and All Thumbs.* Chase's thoughts on the joys of amateur playing are consistent with our own. There is a bit of Zen mixed in here, all to the good, with plenty of hope for the late bloomer.

Chasins, Abram, *Speaking of Pianists . . . ,* New York, NY: Da Capo Press, 1981. Chasins's book is full of entertaining and informative stories about a legion of great pianists. A wealth of critical material abounds here. Rich anecdotes make it a natural follow-up to the Charles Cooke book.

Dubal, David, *Reflections from the Keyboard,* New York, NY: 1984. This is a serious interview book (about 400 full pages). Excellent pianists are included along with a richly detailed index with individual works set forth! Not to give away the plot, but since musicians are notorious for telling stories on one another, I can't resist retailing Bar-Illan's remark about Sol Hurok, who was supposed to have defined a cultural exchange as "when the Russians send us Jews from Odessa and we send them Jews from Odessa." A good pianist's joke.

Fay, Amy, *Music-Study in Germany*, New York, NY: Da Capo Press, 1979. Amy Fay's charming account of her nineteenth-century music studies with Liszt and Tausig is a classic of its kind that is beautifully and warmly written.

Good, Edwin M., *Giraffes, Black Dragons, and Other Pianos*, Stanford, CA: Stanford University Press, 1982. Good is a master describer of sounds and makes the differences between old and new instruments, European and American, large and small, come alive. He captures Bösendorfer and Bluthner particularly well, and he is entertaining besides.

Hildebrandt, Dieter, *Pianoforte—A Social History of the Piano*, with an Introduction by Anthony Burgess, New York, NY: George Braziller, 1988. A fine introduction is provided by that accomplished musician and writer Anthony Burgess to this cultural history of the piano. Largely anecdotal and historical, it still provides a lot of good facts and interesting literary and biographical references. For instance, Clara Schumann's exoneration of her father for his management of her childhood time was most touchingly put when she said, "I will thank him all my life for his so-called cruelty."

Horowitz, Joseph, *Conversations with Arrau*, New York, NY: Alfred A. Knopf, 1982. Mostly interviews with and about Arrau, plus a lengthy discography, this worthwhile book does develop a lot of useful detail for the amateur. The Chopin Preludes are discussed fully, plus there are fascinating details about Arrau's long and successful career. His three hours a day devoted to reading and time given to book and art collecting and walking all help fill out a colorful verbal picture.

Libermann, Alexander, *A Comprehensive Approach to the Piano*. Berkeley, CA: Arif Press, 1984. This series of lectures was delivered by the author at Mills College. One of the last master teachers in the mold of Rubenstein and Horowitz, he conversationally sets forth many of his aids to students of the piano. He is vitally concerned with "what" the pianist wishes to say, rather than the "how" he says it. He thinks little of silent keyboard practice, separate hand practice (unless they "say" something differently), excessive slow practice, and unrealistic tempi. His expression, "anticipated manifest of will," lucidly describes the phenomenon of finger tripping or stumbling that occurs when we rush too precipitously on to the final note of a passage or trill. This is a difficult but worthwhile book to search for. The distributor is Granary Books in New York.

Mach, Elyse, *Great Pianists Speak for Themselves*, New York, NY: Dodd, Mead, 1980. This is another lighter-weight interview book than the above, though fairly enjoyable. It gets out some fairly meaty facts on memorization and that little-discussed topic of chamber music. Ashkenazy's quote on either being born with natural keyboard coordination or not came from this material, although he has probably announced that elsewhere. Not a bad effort.

Marcus, Adele, *Great Pianists Speak*, Neptune, NJ: Paganiniana Publications, 1979. One whose name is usually preceded by the words "The great teacher . . ." gathered together a choice bunch of interviewees (Bachauer, Schnabel, de Larrocha) and squeezed out some good thoughts on slow and silent practice, subtle left pedal work, and a flock of tips on mastering tough passages. No index, but probably no big deal in this more personal context.

Noyle, Linda J., *Pianists on Playing: Interviews with Twelve Concert Pianists*. Metuchen, NJ: Scarecrow Press, 1987. The format smacks of the published thesis, and almost all of the pianists have been interviewed elsewhere and more than once. No matter, because what makes this book work is the uniqueness of the questions since they are all the same. If that sounds like it might be dull, somehow it isn't. The method brings out more depth in a lot of areas, finger position, warmups, breathing, rhythm, health, metronomes, and all the rest. If you don't come away convinced that tone is everything, you've missed the point.

Ristad, Eloise, *A Soprano on Her Head*, Moab, UT: Real People Press, 1982. Another amusing and instructive "head" book like Chase's *Just Being at the Piano*, this viewpoint comes at the problems of the piano from an innovative direction, upside down. That is, it provides a fresh approach to mastering the keyboard.

Schnabel, Arthur, *My Life and Music*, Mineola, NY: Dover Publications, 1988. Assembled from a series of lectures Robert Hutchins talked him into giving at the University of Chicago, these talks convey the master's sensitive thoughts about the piano and, particularly, about music most effectively. You will find his observations about nationalism in piano manufacture applicable to today's instruments. Good words flow about finger and hand position. The maestro is no less interesting when discussing the changes in our society due to the industrial revolution and man's dependence on machinery and its products.

Schonberg, Harold C., *Chamber and Solo Instrument Music*, Westport, CT: Greenwood Press, 1978. On the surface this book appears to be merely a collection of record reviews. However, if you consider that the author is responsible for two editions of *The Great Pianists* and numerous other exemplary works about music and musicians, you might be encouraged to plunge into these record evaluations not only to learn more about the artists but to discover intriguing observations about the compositions that comprise the bulk of the amateur's efforts.

In discussing Schubert's monumental Sonata in B-flat performed by Horowitz, Schonberg writes, "(He) even manages to make the work sound pianistic ... (by) over-romanticiz(ing), with exaggerated pianissimos and fortissimos." Speaking of his beloved Novaes, he writes, "As an illustration of how the piano should be played rather than hammered, this disc is Exhibit A." Throughout are to be found imaginative descriptions of the performances, particularly with reference to interpretation, that can assist in guiding the amateur in his approach to these standard works.

Wilson, Frank R., *Tone Deaf and All Thumbs*, NY: Viking, 1986. Addressing himself to "late-bloomers and non-prodigies," the author employs simplistic humor and farfetched examples to nevertheless lead and stimulate the performer by novel and creative methods. There is plenty written here about rhythm, teachers, love of practice, pedaling, and all else.

Most pianists' libraries contain copies of Mozart's *Letters*, Mozart's biography by Einstein, Charles Rosen's *The Classical Style*, and many others, including authoritative, if fragmentary, works assembled from the writings and notebooks of Joseph Lhevinne, Joseph Hofmann, Walter Geiseking, and Juilliard's Adele Marcus.

As the most vital of the foregoing I would list the Cooke, Dubal, Huneker, Newman, and Whiteside. However, close to these in pianistic interest and valuable insight into what makes a fine musician tick would be Arthur Rubinstein's splendid two-volume biography, *My Young Years* and *My Many Years*. Obviously biographies about other famous composers and pianists make absorbing reading, especially if they are about Chopin and Liszt. These lives guarantee surefire entertainment in the hands of a good biographer. How better to enhance your enjoyment of playing when you are not at the keyboard or listening to music?

The use of basic reference books like Hutcheson and Ferguson can be reinforced by physically gluing on index tabs at places where you are most apt to consult them most frequently. Choose either composers by name or by that part of their works to which you most frequently refer, such as Beethoven and Mozart Sonatas, Chopin Etudes, Brahms Short Pieces, Debussy Preludes, etc.

Other Publications

In days of yore, *Etude* magazine was a periodical that was held in the highest esteem by pianists in the enlightened amateur class. As times have changed, so have such specialty publications. Alas, *Etude* is no more. However, as the traveling gourmand would not be caught dead without his current issue of Gault Millau's *Guide France or a doyen of the kitchen her copy of Gourmet,* a card-carrying amateur pianist will be relieved to know that help is at hand. *The Piano Quarterly* and *Keyboard Classics* do this job between them. *PQ* treats the subject more broadly and sports an appetizing format. *KC* is more utilitarian and slanted toward teachers. Neither, perhaps, is as good as its predecessor, but taken together the pianist is assured a decent flow of interviews, articles, analysis, features, workshops, and examples from actual scores. If you plan to take only one, the nod assuredly goes to the more elegant of the two, *The Piano Quarterly.*

An unlikely area for a pianist's inspiration can spring from the entertainment section of newspapers and magazines. These generally contain advertisements of concerts and critical reviews about piano events and performances that are about to occur or have occurred, not to mention occasional interviews with visiting artists. Even a mere listing of program selections, particularly of shorter pieces, can often provide creative direction for shaping one's personal repertoire. Reviews of concerts usually bring out details of the performance in enough depth to stimulate imagination further. Also there is the possible mention of encore selections, usually short pieces again, which can furnish yet more ideas for personal playing.

All of this sort of piano oriented material, as much as you can get your hands on, serves the single main objective for which we are striving, to help improve, reinforce, and expand our playing.

A new aid to detailed study of a particular piece is possible through the audio tape medium. Paul Badura-Skoda, to name one example—there may be more—offers a Master Class in Mozart's Sonata in A (Köchel No. 331). The whole presentation is beautifully and thoughtfully done and contains much humor and joy. Other such items are obtainable through *Keyboard Classics*.

The Classical Pianist is a pamphlet printed 2 or 3 times annually that lists used classic recordings in 78 and 33⅓ RPM plus copied cassette tapes that are for sale. The material offered hits right at the core of the amateur pianist's interests. All the great works and all the great historic pianists can eventually be found here, including those whose keyboard wizardry exists only on sources dubbed from piano rolls. The pamphlet, including its interesting commentary, is obtained by writing to *The Classical Pianist*, P.O. Box 545, Mundelein, IL, 60060.

In seeking out books from old lists that could be out of print, it would be well to acquaint yourself with *Books in Print*. This useful catalogue of *all* books currently being published is available at the reference desk of your local library and at nonchain book stores. Books are listed by title and author.

BBC Music Guides

The British Broadcasting Company publishes many music guides, several of which deal exclusively with the piano. Authors are different for the various composers and represent amusing and informative writing at its best. A current list includes:

Beethoven Piano Sonatas	Dennis Matthews
Debussy Piano Music	Frank Dawes
Brahms Piano Music	Dennis Matthews
Schubert Piano Sonatas	Phillip Radcliffe
Schumann Piano Music	Joan Chissel

To single out Matthews's booklet on Brahms for one, it is both delightfully anecdotal and richly instructive. There are sufficient notational examples—all quite clearly printed—to provide excellent guideposts for the text without being overwhelming.

In discussing one of the Handel Variations, he says, "they share a Brahmsian tendency to hide the melodic line in an inner part." Of

Number 10 of the Paganini Variations, he says, "The extraordinary harmonic effect of No. 10 derives from long-held appoggiaturas that send off rockets or arpeggios in their own right." And later he adds, "A famous drawing of Brahms by Willy von Beckerath shows the composer enjoying the end of a cigar and playing the piano with his left hand stretched across his right." He suggests that the work being played might have been the "Rhapsody" in G minor and goes on to give a good musical reason for the apparent acrobatics. Delightful writing and superb ideas are contained in these handy booklets.

BBC *Beethoven.* Nowhere is the need for Matthews's insightful prose more keen than in the endless shelves of writings about Beethoven. Here again in the thrifty BBC music guide series, he says the following about one example of the master's (for is not Beethoven the Henry James of music?) early Sonata in F minor, Opus 2, No. 1: "This [Mozart's G minor Symphony, to which he was referring at the time] offers an interesting comparison. Mozart, for all his drama, clinched and rounded off his theme: Beethoven allows it its head, jumps forward to a fortissimo climax in no time at all, falls back exhausted, pauses, develops it more cautiously in another key altogether, and still reaches his second subject in record time."

Such a use of a successful racehorse metaphor should send the reader scurrying off in two directions at once, the first to delve further into the redoubtable Matthews, and second, to attack the hapless Sonata with renewed challenge and regard, and with assuredly no thought that it might be uninteresting "early Beethoven."

Later he offers an opinion as to why the E-flat Sonata is heard so infrequently: "This affectionate, warmhearted sonata is seldom played. Why? Because it ends up so unsensationally on an intimate tender note." Warmhearted—what a thought! One longs to play it right now. To support this urge, based on the knowledge that Beethoven himself loved to play his Sonata in B-flat Major, Opus 26, and particularly the andante movement, wild horses should be incapable of restraining your compulsion to rush to the piano seat. Lest we forget Donald Ferguson's comparable gift in this area, this quote is part of his description of Brahms's Capriccio No. 5 from the estimable Opus 76, "good stuff with which to endure a world too disordered for intellect to untangle. Make a story or not, as you please; but do not suppose that this music represents anything less than a high reality of complex experience."

Stumbling on this marvelous quotation is precisely what I am advocating when I beseech the player to act immediately and enthusiastically on such encounters that often pop up in print. Go to the piano at your earliest opportunity. Snatch the Brahms music from its well-chosen location and *play that capriccio*. Never will you feel greater satisfaction in breaking up the "steely tyranny of light" and, through the ear, approaching "the soul's final secret."

Such is the ability of fine music criticism: to interest, engage, charge, and activate the reader. Ferguson and Matthews vie with Tovey in this. We are eternally in their debt, along with other authors and publications included here for illuminating the path toward these fulfilling musical experiences.

Out-of-Print Book Sources

While many of the vital piano oriented books are currently in print and available through sources previously discussed, it is valuable to be aware of antiquarian bookshops that specialize in books about music. The *AB Bookman's Yearbook* includes these stores that focus on musical literature:

About Music, P.O. Box 31415, San Francisco, CA 94131

Academy Book Store, 10 W. 18th St., New York, NY 10011

Ars Antiqua Books, P.O. Box 437, Bloomfield, CT 06002

Bancroft Book Mews, 86 Sugar Lane, Newtown, CT 06470

Bel Canto Books, P.O. Box 55, Metuchen, NJ 08840

Books and Music, 801 E. Salem, Indianola, IA 50125

Book Marks, 1 E. Pleasant St., Amherst, MA 01266

Book Stop, 3640-A King St., Alexandria, VA 22302

Dorothy Elsberg, Box 178, West Stockbridge, MA 01266

The Footnote, 179 Washington Park, Brooklyn, NY 11205

Little Mermaid, 411 Park St., Upper Montclair, NJ 07043

J and J Lubrano, 39 Hollenbeck Ave., Great Barrington, MA 01230

Sheldon L. Tarakan, 40 Holly Lane, Roslyn Heights, NY 11577.

Conclusion

Choices, choices. Life is made up of choices. To say otherwise is to suggest that life itself provides a fulfillment and all we need to do is to position ourselves like an urn beneath a urinating stone cupid in order to be showered with its bounty.

Wrong.

Not only is life an endless, complex tapestry of choices, it is also a slough of despair for those who would lament lost opportunities, choices not pursued, and paths not taken. It threatens to be a quagmire of perpetual debate over decisions won by narrow margins, parallel regrets, and anguish over alternative choices, and long-faced lamentation over more verdant fields that might have spelled joy and success if only they had been chosen instead.

Business, the professions, the arts, personal involvement, hobbies, ill health, recreation, necessary functions, all fractionalize that wee scrap of waking time we all have available for some part of our manageable lives. Apportioning this smorgasbord is demanding, to say the least. The very process of selection can swallow up the worthy impulse it should be capable of choosing. Our excessively communicative society conspires to overwhelm and annihilate our best-intentioned, avocational goals.

What do most of us do? We succumb. We find the pressing economic, marital, social, familial, and bodily influences too compelling to withstand. The angularities and opacities of life confound our righteous impulses. We are defeated before we have a chance to start. Life does us in. We seem to have no chance to reach for and grasp these worthy goals for which we strive.

Then why is it that a Marie Callender starts a multi-million dollar business by cooking up pies in her homemaker's oven? Why is it that a Steve Jobs turns an IBM monolith on its ear by brainstorming computer marketing ideas with a bunch of bejeaned and T-shirted geniuses who reinvent the electronic world? Are we to think of these types as aberrations and to think of ourselves as too pedestrian or vulnerable to achieve this sort of expressive nirvana?

Actually the establishment of a beachhead commitment in music, provided there exists some early exposure, talent, and yearning, is one of the most challenging and, at the same time, satisfying quests you can undertake.

A satisfying life's work is what everybody is trying to find in one way or another. It is eluding most of us. What we advocate here is to press on vigorously with what you must come to regard as an artistic calling, if you will. You must harness this inclination toward a musical avocation, but do it in a semiprofessional mode and not as merely one of a number of extra-business, extra-recreational choices.

> Did some more sober critic come abroad.
> If wrong, I smiled; if right, I kissed the rod.
> Praises(?), reading, study, are their just pretence,
> And all they want is spirit, taste, and such.
> Commas and points they set exactly right.
> And t'were a sin to rob them of their mite.
> Alexander Pope, "Epistle to Dr. Arbuthnot"
> Lines 157–62

> Blessed is he who has found his work;
> Let him ask no other blessedness.
> Thomas Carlyle, "Past and Present"
> *(The Modern Worker)*

We are that critic. We are that worker. Aside from the bread-winning mold in which we are routinely cast, we are capable of more divine effort, so to speak, or at the very least, more sublimated effort.

Cynically viewed, being an amateur is having to endure those abysmal moments that occur all to frequently, perhaps several times daily, when you are reminded how lousy you are. It is also being allowed an occasional glimpse of a competency and a beauty you never realized you could produce. Such is the reality of amateurism.

I have long thought that when our lives were simpler, those of us who were students worked hard at the business of schooling, attended lectures, read and studied voluminously, wrote papers, took examinations, and only occasionally attaining first-class results. Yet our commitment seemed to leave time for many extracurricular involvements. Why should being an adult foreclose us from this thrill of enhancing study with art? Where is it written that life must be composed of so many jousting, tugging, tumultuous elements that we scarcely have time to draw a tranquil breath from one sunset to the next?

Here in this book we have urged you to adopt an adult vow of commitment to "cast the new aside, and be the first by whom the old is tried," to paraphrase Pope.

If you feel you have an inkling or an urge, a talent, an untapped spring, this is the excuse you have been waiting for to develop your bliss into something large enough to follow.

"Music I heard with you was more than music," is the poignant first line of Conrad Aiken's longing poem, "Bread and Music," and expresses the role of "otherness" that this mystical art can provide.

Discography of Mostly Piano Solo

(On Compact Disc)

Bach

English Suites, Nos. 2 and 3–Ivo Pogorelich. DG 415 480-2
French Suites–Glenn Gould. CBS MK 42267
Goldberg Variations–Glenn Gould. CBS MK 37779
Inventions–Andras Schiff. London 411 974-2
Italian Concerto, Etc.–Alfred Brendel. Philips 412 252-2
Well Tempered Clavichord–Andras Schiff. London 414 388-2

Beethoven

Five Piano Concertos–Rudolph Serkin. Telarc CD-80061
Sonatas–Daniel Barenboim. DG 413 766-2, etc.
Sonatas–Richard Goode. Book of the Month Club Records 31-7510
  Nos. 1 and 2

Brahms

Ballades and Opus 76–Stephen Bishop Kavacevich. Harmonia
  Mundi HMC 901193

Chopin

Andante Spianato and Grande Polonaise (and Misc. including Barcarolle and Berceuse)–Artur Rubinstein. RCA 5617-2RC

Ballades and Scherzos–Vladimir Ashkenazy. London 417 474-2
Etudes–Vlado Perlmuter. Nimbus 5095
Etudes–Maurizio Pollini. DG 413 794-2
Impromptus–Murray Perahia. CBS MK 39708
Nocturnes (Selection)–Daniel Barenboim. DG 415 117-2
Polonaises–Artur Rubinstein. RCA 5615-2
Preludes–Maurizio Pollini. DG 413 796-2
Scherzos and Polonaise-Fantasie–Claudio Arrau. Philips 610-2412
Sonata No. 2–Vlado Perlmuter. Nimbus 5038
Sonatas No. 2 and 3–Maurizio Pollini. DG 415 346-2
Waltzes–Claudio Arrau. Philips 400 025-2

Debussy

Children's Corner–Jacques Rouvier. Denon 33637-7372
Preludes–Alain Plainès. Harmonic 8506-7

Franck

Prelude, Chorale, and Fugue–Shura Cherkassky. Nimbus 5090

Haydn

Sonatas–Alfred Brendel. Philips 412 228-2, etc.

Liszt

Various Albums–Jorge Bolet. London 410 257-2, etc.
Major Selection (Mephisto Waltz, La Campanella, Sonata in
   b)–Minoru Nojima. Reference Recordings 25CD
Various Selections–Andre Watts. Angel CDC-7 47380 2, etc.
Sonata & Concert Etudes–Louis Lortie. Chandos 8548
Sonata–Shura Cherkassky. Nimbus 5045
Sonata–Alfred Brendel. Philips 410 040-2

Mendelssohn

Sonata–Murray Perahia. CBS MK 37838
Songs without Words (Selection)–Andras Schiff. London 421 199-2

Mozart

Sonatas–Mitsuko Uchida. Philips 420 185-2, etc.
Sonata, K, 448 (Duet)–Perahia and Lupu. CBS MK 39511

Mussorgsky

Pictures at an Exhibition–Barry Douglas. RCA 5931-2RC

Rachmaninoff

Preludes–Vladimir Ashkenazy. London 414 417-2

Ravel

Selections–Vlado Perlmuter. Nimbus 5005 (Vols. 1, 2)

Satie

Selections–Pascal Rogé. London 410 220-2

Scarlatti

Sonatas (Selection)–Andras Schiff. Hungaraton HCD 11806-2
Sonatas (Selection)–Alexis Weissenberg. DG 415 511-2

Schubert

Impromptus–Alfred Brendel. Philips 411 040-2
Impromptus–Radu Lupu. London 411 711-2
Sonatas–Alfred Brendel. Philips 411 477-2, etc.
Anthologies–Horowitz, Cherkassky.

Appendix:
List of Music Publishers
and Stores

Boston Music Company
116 Boylston St.
Boston, MA 02100   All publishers

Dale Music Co., Inc.
8240 Georgia Ave.
Silver Springs, MD 20910   All publishers

Carl Fischer, Inc.
62 Cooper Square   Standard repertoire plus
New York, NY 10003   special publications

G. Henle/USA, Inc.
P.O. Box 1753
St. Louis, MO 63043   Henle Publications

(Edwin F. Kalmus)
CPP/Belwin, Inc.
15800 N.W. 48th Avenue
Miami, FL 33014   Kalmus and various

Hal Leonard Publishing Co.
P.O. Box 13819
Milwaukee, WI 53213   Schirmer and all publishers

Music Exchange
151 W. 46th St.
New York, NY 10036   All publishers

Joseph Patelson Music House, Ltd.
160 W. 56th St.   Cortot Salabert Editions
New York, NY 10019   and all publishers

Patti Music Corporation
P.O. Box 1514
Madison, WI 53701   Discount and all publishers

C.F. Peters Corporation
373 Park Avenue South
New York, NY 10016   Editions Peters

Theodore Presser Co.
Bryn Mawr, PA 19010   Foreign and all publishers

Schmitt Music Center
88 South Tenth Street
Minneapolis, MN 55400   All publishers

PIANO EVALUATION AND ESTIMATE SHEET

Customer__Higson_____Ph. #_____
Piano Make_Steinway____#241339_____
Model_A__Finish_Ebony_Case#_D5466___
Date_11-14-86 (Built in 1926)

GENERAL	Good	Needs Service	Needs replacement	Labor cost	Parts cost	Total cost	COMMENTS
1. Agraffes		X					painted
2. Bridges, Pins, Notching	X						scraped/sm. cracks
3. Case Parts	X						good
4. Downbearing							didn't measure
5. Finish & Touch-up	X						
6. Frame	X						
7. Keybed, Spring, Block		X					cln spring; nu felt
8. Legs & Lyre		X					rebuild lyre
9. Pinblock & Tuning Pins	X						oversize tuning pins
10. Plate	X						poor letters
11. Soundboard & Ribs	X						shims + dowel repair
12. Strike Point #88		X					poor hammer align.
13. Strings	X						restrung
14. Trapwork & Levers		X					needs rebuilding
DAMPER ACTION							
15. Centers	X						
16. Damper Felt	X						new
17. Guide Rail & Bushings	X						
18. Heads	X						
19. Regulation		X					uneven lift
20. Springs	X						
21. Stop Rail & Felt			X				original
22. Tray & Felt			X				original
23. Wires							
STACK							
24. Action Rails	X						good
25. Action Spread	X						111 mm - 112 mm
26. Centers		X					tight whippens

STACK (cont.)

Item				Comments
27. Hammers	X			new
28. Knuckles	X			new
29. Reg. Button Punchings			X	original
30. Regulation		X		uneven
31. Shanks & Flanges	X			Teflon (!)
32. Whippens		X	X	original: rebuild or replace

KEYS & KEYFRAME

Item				Comments
33. Backchecks & Leather	X			
34. Backrail Cloth & Punchings			X	Original
35. Balance Pin Hole	X			seems o.k.
36. Bushings		X		borderline
37. Buttons	X			
38. Key Covering	X			new
39. Keyframe & Shift Block		X		replace felt
40. Key Lifter Felt			X	original
41. Key Pins		X		clean + lube
42. Key Regulation	X			height + dip o.k.
43. Sharps	X			new: plastic

MISCELLANEOUS

Item				Comments
44. Cartage				
45. Cleaning				
46. Estimate				
47. Follow-up				
48. Travel Time				
49. Tuning — Shop				
50. Tuning — Home				
51. Voicing		X		uneven

NOTES

Wound strings: 8 singles, 12 doubles (bass)
5 doubles (tenor)

Decay ring time : 29 seconds — bass
23 " — tenor
15 " — midrange
8 " — break area
4 " — treble
3 " — high treble

Estim. Value :
$6,500

Index

Numbers in **boldface** indicate musical examples.